SAP® SuccessFactors: An Introduction into the Talent Management Modules

Pablo Stuardo

Thank you for purchasing this book from Espresso Tutorials!

Like a cup of espresso coffee, Espresso Tutorials SAP books are concise and effective. We know that your time is valuable and we deliver information in a succinct and straightforward manner. It only takes our readers a short amount of time to consume SAP concepts. Our books are well recognized in the industry for leveraging tutorial-style instruction and videos to show you step by step how to successfully work with SAP.

Check out our YouTube channel to watch our videos at
https://www.youtube.com/user/EspressoTutorials.

If you are interested in SAP Finance and Controlling, join us at
http://www.fico-forum.com/forum2/
to get your SAP questions answered and contribute to discussions.

Related titles from Espresso Tutorials:

- ▶ Björn Weber: First Steps in the SAP® Production Processes (PP)
  http://5027.espresso-tutorials.com

- ▶ Sydnie McConnell & Martin Munzel: First Steps in SAP®
  (2nd, extended *edition*)
  http://5045.espresso-tutorials.com

- ▶ Ashish Sampat: First Steps in SAP® Controlling (CO)
  http://5069.espresso-tutorials.com

- ▶ Ann Cacciottolli: First Steps in SAP® Financial Accounting (FI)
  http://5095.espresso-tutorials.com

- ▶ Janet Salmon & Claus Wild: First Steps in SAP® S/4HANA Finance
  http://5149.espresso-tutorials.com

- ▶ Claudia Jost: First Steps in the SAP® Purchasing Processes (MM), Second Edition
  http://5166.espresso-tutorials.com/

- ▶ Bert Vanstechelman: The SAP® HANA Deployment Guide
  http://5289.espresso-tutorials.com

Pablo Stuardo
SAP® SuccessFactors: An Introduction into the Talent Management Modules

ISBN:	978-1-71890-979-3
Editor:	Alice Adams
Cover Design:	Philip Esch
Cover Photo:	© istockphoto.com | filadendron # 527617369
Interior Book Design:	Johann-Christian Hanke

All rights reserved.

1st Edition 2018

© Espresso Tutorials GmbH, Gleichen 2018

URL: *www.espresso-tutorials.com*

Feedback
We greatly appreciate any kind of feedback you have concerning this book. Please mail us at *info@espresso-tutorials.com*.

Table of Contents

Preface

This book is part of an introductory series of books on SAP SuccessFactors.

SAP is one of the most successful enterprise software providers in the world, and one of its biggest products, SAP SuccessFactors, is the leading HR software within the ecosystem. With this book, you will receive a comprehensive introduction to what SAP SuccessFactors is, what it does, and details on the main features and functions available in the Talent Management suite.

Unlike other technical books, this particular book has been written for professionals with limited experience and knowledge of SAP SuccessFactors. The book covers basic features and functionality available without covering configuration or technical details.

The audience for this content are executives and professionals in the HR space considering implementing SAP SuccessFactors, or who want to learn more about this technology, to students about to graduate who would like to learn more about this exciting industry.

I have divided this book into chapters that cover a module within the system which cover a group of features and functionality that provide solutions to talent management processes; you will learn more about modules very soon.

We have added a few icons to highlight important information. These include:

Tips

Tips highlight information that provides more details about the subject being described and/or additional background information.

Attention

Attention notices highlight information that you should be aware of when you go through the examples in this book on your own.

Finally, a note concerning the copyright: all screenshots printed in this book are the copyright of SAP SE. All rights are reserved by SAP SE. Copyright pertains to all SAP images in this publication. For the sake of simplicity, we do not mention this specifically underneath every screen-shot.

1 Introduction

Everyone working at large organizations knows that within each company there are many different business functions. A business function would be defined as the area of expertise and similar business actions and processes that need to exist to add value within an organization. For example, Marketing would be one, Finance another, Information Technology, Human Resources, etc.

In today's world it is not news that all these business functions have to be integrated and "talk" to each other in order to maintain a minimum level of efficiency and remain competitive. There are no longer the days where the left hand does not work with or know what the right hand does.

You might have some knowledge of enterprise resource planning (ERP) systems so I will not explain what it is or the overall benefits. However I do want to briefly discuss Human Resources (HR) within an ERP system, which is considered one of the largest back office functions in any organization.

1.1   Human Resources

SAP is an enterprise application software company. The name is an acronym for System, Applications and Products in Data Processing. SAP's cloud solution for Human Resources software is called SAP Success-Factors.

There are two key elements of HR processes and data: Core HR and Talent Management. Figure 1.1 illustrates this concept as represented in the SuccessFactors system.

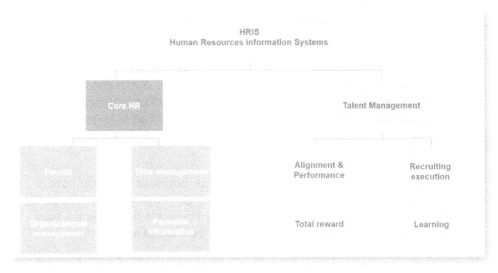

Figure 1.1: HRIS processes and data

As a foundation for SAP SuccessFactors, you should understand that all these HR elements, can be handled by the SAP Human Capital Management (HCM) module.

Some may argue about how useful or robust the SAP HCM platform is for talent management processes; however, the key takeaway is that HR business functions are no longer just time management and payroll.

Quite a bit of emphasis needs to be added to HR systems by including and supporting complex talent management business processes. And because of this, SAP recognized that these needed to be developed quickly and acquired a company called SuccessFactors in 2012.

Commonly accepted name for SAP SuccessFactors

 Although the official name is SAP SuccessFactors, throughout the book we will just refer to SuccessFactors as it is commonly referred within the industry.

1.2   Objectives

To begin building a complete framework of SuccessFactors, let's look at some scenarios, but this is merely the "tip of the iceberg" of what it offers. Imagine:

▶ Accessing an employee's personal information and being able to see or edit any information that you have authorization to see/edit.

▶ Look at a very intuitive company organization chart.

▶ Filling out performance reviews and maintaining a constant conversation with your team about performance and development.

▶ Planning salary increases and variable pay for your team.

▶ Understanding your career path, desired next position, and see exactly what qualifications and competencies you need to be considered for it.

▶ Taking learning courses, on your laptop or on your phone/tablet, which are directly linked with your current position as well as positions and roles you aspire to move to.

▶ Filling job requisitions to find the best candidates for your team.

▶ Performing onboarding functions to welcome new hires.

▶ Having the ability to report on everything just mentioned and much more.

The purpose of this book is to provide a comprehensive overview of all Talent Management modules in SuccessFactors, as shown on the right side of Figure 1.1. Because of the amount of content to be reviewed, I have divided the content into two books.

This first book focuses on the talent management process of an employee cycle:

▶ Basic Employee Profile data

▶ Tracking goals and performance

▶ Employee Development

▶ Total reward

▶ Succession planning

▶ Basic reporting

The second book covers recruiting execution and learning:

▶ Marketing and recruiting for a job

▶ Applying for a job and being onboarded

▶ Employee learning

Once you have read these books, you will have a full understanding of SuccessFactors and the solutions it offers to common HR business problems in talent management.

Now that you have a very basic idea of SuccessFactors, let's look at how this book is structured.

1.3 Overview

If you have been in the Human Resources environment and/or an HRIS (Human Resources Information System) professional for some short period of time, most likely you know about SuccessFactors. However, at the same time, unless you have used the system, you don't really know much about it.

When I ask the question, what is SuccessFactors? I very often hear responses like: "it has to do with HR, right?" or "I think you do your performance evaluations there..." Just to put it in some context, these answers come from professionals in the HR space.

In addition, when asking the question to people outside the HR business function or HRIS (other business functions, or smaller companies), it is very likely that people have no idea of what SuccessFactors is.

This book has been written to provide a source of education about what SuccessFactors is.

The purpose is to help educate people from Chief Human Resources Officer (CHRO) or Chief Information Officer (CIO) down the hierarchy who are contemplating buying the software and/or learning more about it. It also helps HRIS professionals who are looking to transition to SuccessFactors, students about to graduate who are looking to get started in a very exciting and fast-paced industry working with SuccessFactors, and everyone in between.

In this book you will learn the following:

▶ What SuccessFactors is?

▶ What does it do?

▶ What are its benefits?

▶ How can the system add value to your organization?

You will acquire an in-depth and detailed overview of SuccessFactors and its Talent Management modules, which itself is extremely important in today's corporate HR world.

Don't worry. If you don't have any idea of what SuccessFactors is, then this book is for you. For additional context, by reading this book you will understand how SuccessFactors can help run your organization better with talent management.

It will help in building better processes for recruiting execution (part 2), defining clear and consistent alignment and performance processes, building a strong framework of a learning organization that pays for performance, and much more.

At the beginning of this book we divided HR into key elements as seen in Figure 1.1: Core HR on the left, and Talent Management on the right. In these books we will be covering what you see under Talent Management in Figure 1.1.

1.4   History

SAP SuccessFactors was founded in 2001 by Lars Dalgaard and Aaron Au, in San Francisco, California. About six years later, the company went public on NASDAQ with the symbol SFSF (even today, the acronym SFSF is used to refer to SuccessFactors).

SuccessFactors initially started mainly as a performance management system to help companies do their performance reviews and compensation planning as well as track goals and development objectives.

However, it very quickly grew into different areas within human resources (HR), with the acquisition of Danish company YouCalc, which brought enhanced reporting capabilities, and Jobs2Web to enhance recruiting execution (more in part 2) among others.

Days before acquiring Jobs2Web, in December 2011, SAP acquired SuccessFactors. However, SuccessFactors remained an independent entity for organizational and operational purposes under the name of "SuccessFactors, an SAP company".

Now the official name is "SAP SuccessFactors", but in the industry it is acceptable to just say "SuccessFactors" to refer to the company and its products.

SuccessFactors has become the undisputed leader in human capital management and talent management cloud solutions in the world, across all industries.

It has the vision to provide a system that delivers global HR solutions and also engages employees by providing a highly interactive and robust system. This system is designed to work with everyone. It is a solution that is easy to use and manage.

We live in a world in which people, and employees in particular, are very disengaged regardless of the fact that we have more communication channels than ever.

Also, the competition among talent is as aggressive as it has ever been, and the opportunities that arise by jumping to other organizations are really winning the battle against employee retention. More than ever, people are leaving their jobs; people no longer stay with the same company for decades.

SuccessFactors is here to help. By reading this book you will have a full understanding about how the system can help you with your talent management practices.

Next, we will cover more details of what you can expect.

1.5   Modules

The SuccessFactors suite is composed of many modules that represent a group of talent management processes and functions. Next you will learn about each of the areas covered in these books.

> **Modules not included in this book**
>
> I have listed the modules below in the logical employee cycle; however, please keep in mind that modules related to recruiting execution and learning are not contained in this book.

1.5.1   Recruiting management (Part 2)

This module is all about the main features and functionality in recruiting management, such as candidate profile, applicant status, job application, interview central and scheduling, job requisitions, employee referral, offer approvals and letters, integrations, and more.

1.5.2   Recruiting marketing (Part 2)

This one addresses recruiting marketing including career sites, career site builder, recruiting dashboard, candidate experience, marketing central, and integration with recruiting management.

1.5.3   Onboarding (Part 2)

Learn about the main features and functionality of onboarding, such as onboarding process, offboarding, crossboarding, U.S. compliance requirements (I-9 and E-Verify), panels and forms, mobile capabilities, and integration with recruiting management and HRIS.

15

1.5.4   Employee profile

In this module you learn about the main features and functionality regarding the employee profile, including what it is, the value it offers, and the concept of views, portlets and fields to store employee data.

1.5.5   Career development

This module covers the main features and functionality in career development. Learn what it can offer your organization, templates to track development goals, career worksheet, career path, and integration with the learning module.

1.5.6   Learning (Part 2)

The module on learning describes its main features and functionality, including

courses, quizzes, curricula, gamification (in employee learning), content management, cross-integration with other modules and third-party vendors, and much more.

1.5.7   Goals

Learn the main features and functionality for goals, such as goals sheets to track performance goals, goals execution including meeting agenda, execution map and status report, and its cross-integration points.

1.5.8   Performance

This module highlights the main features and functionality related to performance, covering performance appraisal forms, workflows, continuous performance, and more.

1.5.9   Calibration

The calibration module explains its main features and functionality for the calibration process, compensation, succession, performance, templates and sessions.

1.5.10 Compensation

In the compensation module, you will learn what it offers your organization, with compensation planning templates, budgets, guidelines, workflows, eligibility rules, group assignments, compensation groups, statements, and more.

1.5.11 Variable pay

This module reviews variable pay, including what it does, conversion tables, bonus calculation options, processing bonus payout, bonus forecasting, and more.

1.5.12 Succession

Here you will learn about all the functionality of succession management such as succession nomination process, position management, position org chart, matrix grid reports, talent pools, and talent search.

1.5.13 Security

SuccessFactors takes security very seriously. Learn all about role-based permissions (RBP) as the foundation of its security framework.

1.5.14 Reporting

Learn the basics of the reporting capabilities within SuccessFactors, including ad-hoc reports, dashboards, and more.

1.6 Updates

An important concept in understanding SuccessFactors is how the system evolves.

One of the main reasons to embrace cloud software like SuccessFactors, is that the degree of customization is minimal.

By having minimal customization, we know that any updates or patches that are pushed to the system should not break anything since it would be a prepackaged solution.

This concept is extremely powerful in my opinion because companies pay license fees and always get the most up-to-date features and functionality (or at least the option to enable them or not), instead of the very costly and time consuming process of maintaining the entire system on your own.

SuccessFactors manages updates and patches with quarterly releases every three months. Thus companies are potentially getting problems fixed and/or new functionality that can solve a business process.

In addition to having an upgrade of the system every three months, it's even better to know that the different product teams get their ideas from clients! SuccessFactors product development takes very seriously any issue, comment or concern that clients bring up in the SuccessFactors community.

SuccessFactors community as a rich source of knowledge

 The SuccessFactors community used to be the official forum for SuccessFactors users and partners. However, it has quickly evolved into an extremely rich and powerful source of knowledge about anything related to SuccessFactors, from Q&A forums, best practices advice, training and development, to product updates, and more.

There are several concepts that compose the quarterly release process.

1.7   Quarterly releases

As mentioned above, these releases push different elements to the system. These are separated into four types of features:

► Universal

► Admin Center opt-in

► Provisioning opt-in

► Opt-out

Let's look at each of these now.

1.7.1   Universal

These are features that are pushed to the system with every release. Normally these are user interface (UI) changes, or other minor fixes. With this type of feature administrators do not have the option to decide whether they want them in their system or not; they will get them no matter what.

1.7.2   Admin Center opt-in

These are features that become available in the system for them to be enabled or configured by each company administrator in the Admin Center. We will learn about Admin Center in Chapter 2.

1.7.3   Provisioning opt-in

These are features that can only be enabled in Provisioning, which in a nutshell means that only SAP SuccessFactors support or a partner can enable them.

1.7.4 Opt-out

These are features that automatically get enabled in the system, just like Universal; however, you as client, do have the opportunity to "turn off" the feature.

1.7.5 Release process

As a general overview of the release process, about a month before each release, each product team shares high-level and detail documentation about every new feature and functionality coming for each module.

Moreover, they host webinars for each module to explain the main new features and functionality coming up in the release along with offering a question-and-answer section for attendees. These webinars are recorded so people can go back for review or reference.

Product teams

 Product teams are the groups that manage, from a development perspective, each module within Success-Factors. They are the ones who basically design the system, ensure quality, and work with learning teams to produce documentation.

The fact that this happens about a month in advance allows plenty of time for administrators to understand and get familiar with new potential changes.

You might be thinking that three months is not very much time to absorb and manage all changes. However, no change is so big that it would change a business process or would have great visibility between one release and another.

For anything that is major, SuccessFactors normally announces years in advance.

Also, the majority of the changes are opt-in, which means that each company administrator will have the option to enable them in the system whenever the organization is ready.

1.8 Provisioning

Provisioning is known as the back-end of SuccessFactors. This system allows consultants to manage, upload and download XML code for the different modules, in addition to most of the configuration to enable different features and functionality across the suite.

In addition, Provisioning is the place where "technical" configuration would be performed like single sign-on (SSO), automatic jobs creation, etc.

With Provisioning, consultants have access to enable and configure any new feature and functionality that is not available in the "Upgrade Center". You can see Upgrade Center in Figure 1.2. Notice how admin opt-in upgrades can be selected by clicking on each name under several categories: important, recommended, and optional.

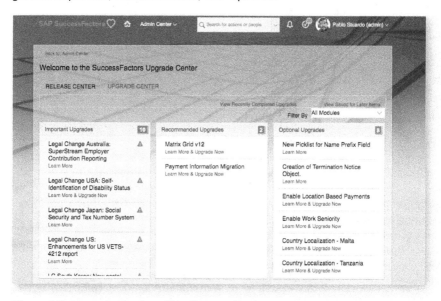

Figure 1.2: Upgrade Center within SuccessFactors

The system is smart enough to only display upgrades that are relevant to your particular system. This means that if you do not have a particular module, let's say recruiting, you would not see any upgrades related to that particular module.

1.9   Who has access to Provisioning?

Because of the power that Provisioning offers, access to it is restricted to only SuccessFactors consultants. It is important to understand that not even customers have access to Provisioning; only consultants do.

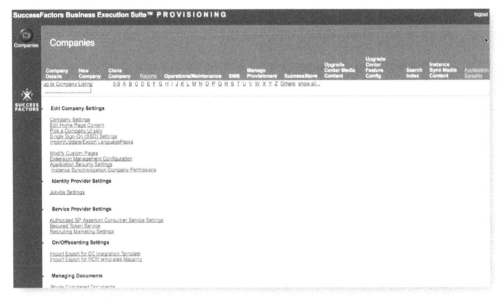

Figure 1.3: Provisioning Main Screen of Settings

For a consultant to have access to Provisioning, they have to follow these guidelines:

▶ Be employed by a consulting company that is in good standing as a partner of SuccessFactors.

▶ The consultant must have a minimum of one SuccessFactors certification, and it must be up-to-date.

▶ Each customer has to explicitly authorize the consulting partner and the consultant with SAP for access to Provisioning.

As you might already see, Provisioning is an extremely powerful tool; since SuccessFactors takes security very seriously, it ensures that anyone who accesses the back end of the system has the necessary credentials and understanding of the system in order to minimize risks.

In Figure 1.3 I have included an image of the settings available on one of the Provisioning screens so you see how it looks, but we will not explore more about it at this point.

1.10 Summary

To summarize, you should now have an understanding of the following in SuccessFactors:

- ▶ Recruiting enables you to create an engaging candidate experience and recruiting process. (Part 2)

- ▶ Onboarding provides a single point of access for new hires even before day 1. Managers can onboard new hires with simple tools at any place and time. (Part 2)

- ▶ With Performance and Goals, users ensure consistent feedback, with more accurate and fair assessment of employee performance.

- ▶ Learning enables everyone to be both student and teacher. (Part 2)

- ▶ Compensation streamlines planning and provides insight for total rewards management.

- ▶ Succession and Development help ensure talent retention by making it easier to identify successors and help employees take responsibility for their own careers.

Ready to dig deeper into each SuccessFactors module and see what the system can offer you? Before you continue and read Chapter 2, I have one final thought; although I divided the book with each module in a chapter, you will notice that one of the beauties about SuccessFactors is that everything is connected and data is consumed and flows across different modules at all times.

Technically you can jump to a specific chapter if you are interested in learning about just one particular module. However, I suggest at least in the beginning to follow the suggested order, which is based on the sequence of events in the logical employee cycle. We are skipping some modules that will be discussed in part 2 of this book series.

Let's go to Chapter 2 to learn more about the SuccessFactors overall platform.

2 Platform & Employee Profile

In Chapter 1, you learned the very basic concept of what SuccessFactors is, a little history as of how SuccessFactors got started and evolved, and about the structure of these books and what I will cover about SuccessFactors Talent Management modules.

This chapter will describe the basics of the platform, as well as the Employee Profile, which is an extremely important module since it brings many other modules together.

Let's take a look at what the SuccessFactors platform looks like.

2.1   Platform overview

The first step to start learning about SuccessFactors is to have access to the system. Since SuccessFactors is a cloud solution it is accessed via a web browser.

The most commonly used browsers that are compatible with SuccessFactors are:

▶   Mozilla Firefox

▶   Google Chrome

▶   Microsoft Windows Internet Explorer

▶   Microsoft Edge

▶   Apple macOS Safari

SuccessFactors instance

 A SuccessFactors instance is simply your SuccessFactors system.

Depending on which data center your SuccessFactors instance is hosted, you will have a different URL that you would use to access.

When SuccessFactors is implemented, your partner will let you know exactly which URL you need to access the system.

A user will enter the Company ID, which is how the system will know the company you are trying to access, and then you will enter your Username and Password like shown on Figure 2.1, just like any other cloud system you might have already used.

Data centers are assigned based on geographical location

 If your company is based in the US, most likely your instance will be hosted in one of the data centers located physically in the United States. Same for Europe, Asia, etc. Normally data centers are assigned based on geographical location of the main company offices.

Figure 2.1: SuccessFactors login page sample

Notice in Figure 2.1—a sample of the login page, how there is a background image and the SuccessFactors logo.

The majority of images in this book are taken from my personal SuccessFactors demo system, so there are several items I have "customized" to match my preferences.

Look and feel of the system

 I do switch between different themes to make a point of how this affects the look and feel of the system.

The background image and logo of course will be adjusted to match your company's brand if desired.

At this point I would like to pause to point out that the majority of companies who use SuccessFactors take advantage of Single Sign-On (SSO) capabilities, which SuccessFactors supports.

By using SSO, the SuccessFactors URL for your company would be hosted in your SSO provider, which means that users would never have to enter their SuccessFactors credentials (username/password).

They would just simple login into their computer, or their "company portal", or into whatever SSO architecture they have, and they would get access to everything, including SuccessFactors, by just entering their "master" credentials once.

Depending on whether you are using regular access to the system by going to a specific URL and then entering your username and password, or taking advantage of SSO technology, the first page you will see (landing page) will be the SuccessFactors home page.

2.1.1 Home page

The home page will be the landing page every time any user enters the system.

Go directly to Admin Center

 If you are a SuccessFactors administrator, you can configure the system so that once you log in, it will take you directly to Admin Center. More on Admin Center later on.

The home page, as pages for all modules in the system can be "themed" according to your company brand, including the logo.

As shown in Figure 2.2, you will see your company logo, then two menus, which we will discuss in detail later in this chapter.

Figure 2.2: SuccessFactors home page sample

The core items on the home page are called "tiles". Let's learn more about them.

2.1.2 Tiles

Tiles, as shown in Figure 2.2, are squared-shaped items that contain some type of information.

The idea behind tiles is to offer users a dashboard all on one screen in which they can see, navigate and monitor a huge range of items across the suite.

It is important to understand that the home page is quite flexible. Tiles can be dragged and dropped into different positions within the screen and their names can be changed.

Tiles can be configured in various ways:

▶ Mandatory for all users (all users will see that particular tile).

▶ Optional, which means that each user has the ability to hide any tile that is not mandatory.

▶ Dynamic, which means that the system would only display tiles that are relevant to each user. For example, the "Manage My Team" tile would only display to users who actually have direct reports. Anyone without direct reports would never see the tile.

Figure 2.3: Manage My Team tile in the SuccessFactors home page

The majority of tiles shown in Figure 2.2 and Figure 2.3 are standard tiles, which means that they are automatically enabled when each SuccessFactors module is implemented.

29

SuccessFactors also supports the ability to create custom tiles. A clear example is the Goal Status tile shown in Figure 2.4.

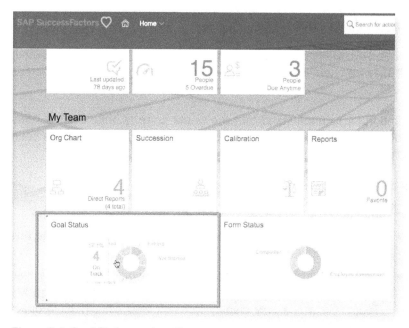

Figure 2.4: Goal Status custom tile

This is a custom tile that was built with a SuccessFactors Dashboard coming from the basic reporting module, and showcases the status of goals in my team's goal plan.

We will dig much deeper into SuccessFactors Dashboards later in this book; however, I want to show a bigger image of this dashboard now.

Imagine I am clicking on the tile in my home page. It will automatically increase the size for better use as shown in Figure 2.5.

Notice how the home page is still behind, but I can see the tile enlarged with some extra information such as which goals are on track, postponed, behind and not started in my team.

Figure 2.5: Goal Status dashboard

Custom tiles can become very useful, and your creativity is the limit. Some innovative custom tiles I have seen in the past include:

▶ Tile that has text with a reminder to complete performance review forms. Let's not forget that this will be displayed in the home page, so every time a user logs into the system they will see the tile.

▶ Tile with an embedded video of the company's leadership showcasing something.

▶ Tile with a survey.

▶ Tile with custom reports as shown in Figure 2.5

Now let's spend the next few sections exploring some of the standard tiles offered in the system.

ToDo

The "ToDo" section let's each user knows which actions they have pending in the system. For example, as shown in Figure 2.6, the section includes tiles that need attention and action.

Figure 2.6: ToDo tiles

The purpose of each tile

After you finish this book, you will understand exactly what each tile does. Standard tiles are fully integrated with other modules in the system; therefore, once you know each module and its processes, all standard tiles become intuitive.

Still in Figure 2.6 let's review the three tiles available:

▶ **Update Your Status**: This tile belongs to the Performance module, particularly involving continuous performance. The tile is telling the user to update the status of the last meeting with their manager in which performance was discussed.

▶ **Review Performance**: This one also belongs to the Performance module and tells the user there are fifteen performance evaluations still to be completed.

▶ **Plan Compensation**: This is part of the Compensation module and it tells the user there are three employees who they are responsible for compensation planning.

Dynamic tiles

All tiles in the system are dynamic, which mean that once a user clicks on them, they are taken directly to the page in which they need to perform the action.

As you can see, most standard tiles are very intuitive. Let's explore a few more.

My Team

The "My Team" section contains all tiles related to a user's team. As mentioned earlier the system is smart enough to know that if a particular user does not have a team (direct reports), this section would never display.

As shown in Figure 2.7, there are several more tiles that are very useful. Let's learn more about some of them:

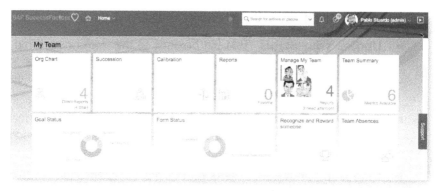

Figure 2.7: My Team tile in the SuccessFactors home page

▶ **Org Chart**: This tile allows a user to navigate directly to the company's org chart, and see where the user is in the org chart and all their direct reports. From there the user can navigate up or down the hierarchy. More to come on the company's org chart later in this chapter.

▶ **Manage My Team**: This is probably one of my favorite tiles. It allows a user to click and see a summary of the team including, but not limited, to what the employee is working on (data coming from Continuous Performance) and To-Dos, in addition to basic information as seen in Figure 2.8.

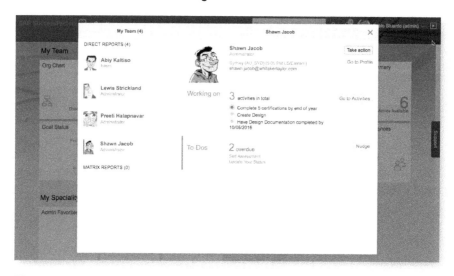

Figure 2.8: My Team tile expanded

> ▶ **Team Summary**: This one is very similar to Manage My Team, but a bit more robust. As shown in Figure 2.9, a user would still be able to see the team, but then on the left side of the screen, the manager in this case can navigate to other screens and see module-specific information.

Figure 2.9: Team View tile

We have reviewed tiles that remind you what to do, and those that offer information about your team, but SuccessFactors is a system for all employees; therefore, let's explore the My Info set of tiles.

My Info

Of course every user is a key component of the system in order for SuccessFactors to add any value; and more critically, your information is very important.

The My Info section in Figure 2.10 includes all tiles relevant to the user on their home page. Let's take a look at some of them:

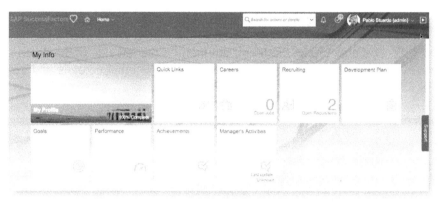

Figure 2.10: My Info tile in the SuccessFactors home page

▶ **My Profile**: This tile takes the user to the Employee Profile module (we will talk extensively about Employee Profile later in this
chapter), but I always like to make the analogy of employee profile being like your "employment folder" with all kind of docu-
ments relevant to you.

▶ **Quick Links**: This allows users to click and review any quick link
the user had previously marked as either "Favorite" or "Available" for quick navigation.

If we take a look at Figure 2.11, we see there are four quick links.
Imagine I am new to the organization. Those four links can be
very useful while I am "learning the ropes" in my new position.

Figure 2.11: Quick Links tile expanded

▶ **Careers**: This allows easy navigation to any internal role that I might be applying to. If a user clicks on it, they will be taken to the Careers section within, where the person can review the status of the positions he/she has applied internally and much more.

▶ **Recruiting**: This enables you to review the status of any open position the user might have in his/her team. The tile belongs in Recruiting.

▶ **Development**: This allows users to easily navigate to their development plan.

▶ **Goals**: Makes it easy to navigate to their goals plan.

▶ **Performance**: Here users get to their performance evaluations.

▶ **Achievements**: With this users can track their achievements. This tile belongs to Continuous Performance.

At this point, I am sure you have a very good understanding of what tiles are, and how powerful they can be.

We learned that tiles are the core of the SuccessFactors home page, and that standard tiles are associated with different modules of the suite, and that the system also allows administrators to configure custom tiles.

Let's continue learning about the home page by understanding the different menus the page offers.

2.1.3   Menus

As mentioned earlier, the home page will be the landing page for all users. In the home page, tiles are available to navigate to different modules of the system, but there are also two very important menus to understand.

Home menu

The home menu, is located in the upper left corner of the screen as shown on Figure 2.12. This menu allows users to navigate to all available modules.

Figure 2.12: Home menu in SuccessFactors home page

The home menu is probably the menu used the most by users in the entire suite.

If we look at Figure 2.12, we can clearly see that each option represents a module on its own.

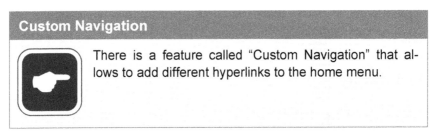

Custom Navigation

There is a feature called "Custom Navigation" that allows to add different hyperlinks to the home menu.

In my system I have implemented almost all modules available in SuccessFactors; that is why the menu has so many options.

Something to always keep in mind is the whole security concept that governs the system.

Of course security is such a huge and important item that I am dedicating a chapter on its own later in book 1; if someone does not have access to something in the system, the user would never even see the options. For example, if the general population of users do not have authorization to access Recruiting because they are not recruiters, the "Recruiting" option would not display.

If we look at Figure 2.13, we are in the same system but logged in as a different user who does not have as much authorization to access all modules as myself (main administrator), therefore, the options available in the Home Menu will be limited compared to Figure 2.12.

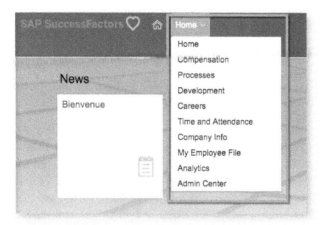

Figure 2.13: Home menu with limited access to certain modules

The home menu is the most popular menu among users because it allows direct access to any of the modules the user has access to; however, there is another very important menu in the home page called the name menu.

Name menu

The name menu can be found toward the upper right corner of the screen, where the user's name and title are displayed as shown in Figure 2.14.

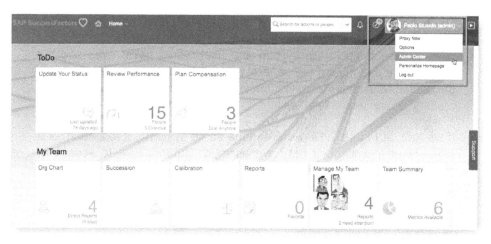

Figure 2.14: Name Menu in SAP SuccessFactors Home Page

This menu contains five very important items in the system for users who have the right authorizations. Let's review all five of them:

▶ **Proxy now**: Proxy is an extremely powerful functionality that allows a user (with proper permissions) to act on behalf of someone else in the system. For example, let's say that I am an administrator, and a business partner calls and tells me she is not able to see the company's org chart. I can "proxy" as this person and see exactly what she sees in efforts to recreate the issue.

An analogy I always like to mention to explain proxy in SuccessFactors is like having IT support connect remotely to your machine. Once they get into your local computer, they are able to act just like you were the one using it.

Because this function is so powerful, security for a proxy should always be taken very seriously. We would hate for anyone to be changing performance scores or even compensation awards of people, or accessing sensitive employee data.

▶ **Options**: This menu option is available to every user of the system. It allows a user to perform different actions, shown in Figure 2.15, with the main ones being:

▶ Change password

▶ Define security questions

▶ Manage email notification preferences

▶ Change language

▶ Accessibility settings

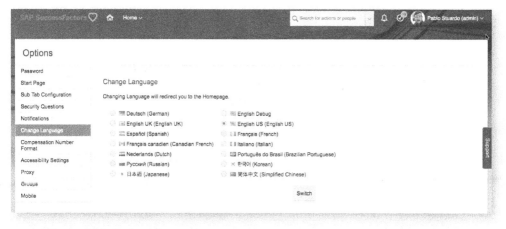

Figure 2.15: Options from name menu

▶ **Admin Center**: This option allows administrators to navigate to Admin Center, which is where most of the configuration and administration of SuccessFactors happens. We will discuss more details later in this chapter.

▶ **Personalize homepage**: This allows users to change the layout and add or hide tiles on their home page.

▶ **Logout**: Here the user would log out of the system.

Language

Now that we are talking about different options for users, it is critical for everyone to understand that SuccessFactors is fully capable of not only translating different languages, but also localizing the suite.

To give some background, companies are global. Employees are located in different countries, with different languages, and different item specifics to each country, such as identification number (ID) format for each country, or address format.

41

SuccessFactors offers full localization for different countries, which becomes very relevant in the Core HR suite and onboarding (with compliance information), but in Talent Management it is very critical too.

Just to give an example, imagine we are launching thousands of performance forms, which we will learn more about later in this book 1.

We do not want to maintain a performance template for each single country. We want to standardize the process in such a way that only one template is designed and forms are "copied" from that template automatically for everyone, regardless of where they are located at or which language they speak.

Different template structures based on different locations

 It is absolutely possible to have different template structures based on different locations, which can become handy for decentralized organizations, however, always the best practice is to have as much of an standardized system and process as possible.

SuccessFactors can handle this. Anything that is standard in the system for text will automatically translate to more than 48 different languages including special characters.

At this point, imagine anything you are doing for performance, compensation, recruiting, etc. Same process, same templates, same ecosystem, but regardless of the physical location, everyone gets to collaborate in a centralized platform in their own language.

In addition to translation and localization, notifications are a huge component of SuccessFactors. Let's learn more about them.

2.1.4 Notifications

Obviously at this point, everyone should understand that SAP SuccessFactors is a system fully driven by processes, but more important, by people.

Because of that, it is important to have a strong communication platform that can let stakeholders in the different processes know what's happening.

SuccessFactors is a system that is very notification-driven. I would say that all modules in the system involve some type of notification.

When we talk about notifications, we mean email notifications. I can think of many potential notifications that users can get such as:

▶ Welcome messages for new users

▶ Password changes

▶ Recruiting notifications

▶ Anytime a document or form, such as performance, compensation, etc. gets generated

▶ Anytime someone routes a form

▶ Anytime someone completes a form

▶ Anytime a goal is created

▶ Anytime a status report on each goal is produced

▶ Anytime an achievement is tracked

▶ Anytime a report is ready to be viewed

▶ Anytime someone is late to do something—remember the ToDo notifications

This list is just a very small sample of the potential hundreds of notifications available in the system, which are triggered by each module.

Something to always keep in mind is that every single notification in the system is managed independently, allowing administrators to either enable or disable the notifications in such a way that this becomes relevant to the culture and processes or the organization; in addition, the content of each notification can also be modified.

Talking about organizations, let's jump into what SuccessFactors offers about company information among other things.

2.1.5   Company information

HR's biggest "asset" is people. Therefore, because of the importance of this, there are some features available in the system to allow people to view certain aspects of the organization from a human capital point of view. At the end of the day, it would be a shame for this HR system to not support basic functions.

Some of these functions are taken for granted, like having a visual of the company's org chart. In my experience it is rather surprising that some of the tools we are about to learn about are not necessarily available in every organization.

Org chart

The company org chart is such a simple and important concept. This feature allows users to look the hierarchical structure of the organization. In Figure 2.16 we can clearly see how the company org chart looks.

Figure 2.16: Company org chart

In Figure 2.16 we can see how I can see myself, Pablo Stuardo, and all my direct reports in a hierarchical image.

Notice also how my photo will always display in addition to my name, last name and title.

The SuccessFactors org chart also allows users to search for people. In Figure 2.17 I am searching for Carla Grant. Once a user starts typing, the results that match will start appearing.

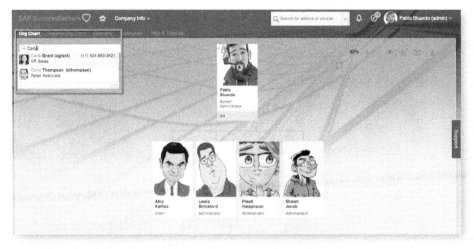

Figure 2.17: Searching for someone in the company org chart

Users can actually open more than one relationship level at once. As seen in Figure 2.18, there are three levels of the hierarchy open.

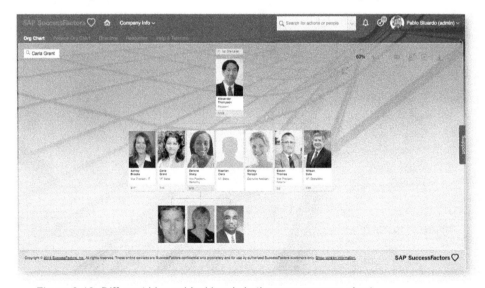

Figure 2.18: Different hierarchical levels in the company org chart

45

One function here in the org chart that is actually very cool and handy is the ability to click on someone's image and seen what is called the "quick card".

The SuccessFactors quick card shows basic information about an employee, in addition to offering the ability to take some action on the employee as shown in Figure 2.19. Some of these actions include:

- ► View employee details
- ► Add a note
- ► Give a badge
- ► See employee compensation
- ► See employee performance history
- ► Succession status
- ► and much more

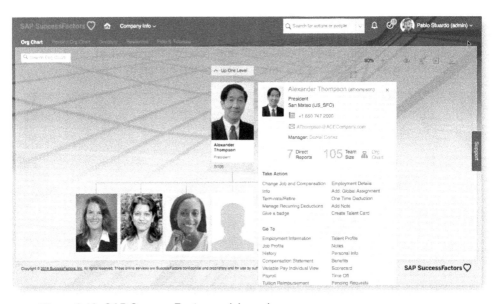

Figure 2.19: SAP SuccessFactors quick card

In addition to the functions discussed, the SucessFactors org chart supports:

► Having direct reports and matrix reports
► Export the org chart (that has been selected) as an
  ► Image
  ► PDF

► Print org chart

Although the SuccessFactors org chart is very often used as a directory, the system does offer a company directory. Let's learn more about it next.

Directory

The company directory is a rather self-explanatory concept. It is a tool that allows users to look up someone and get certain information about the person in the company. As seen in Figure 2.20, a user can enter keywords such as name or title or simply information about someone in the search fields.

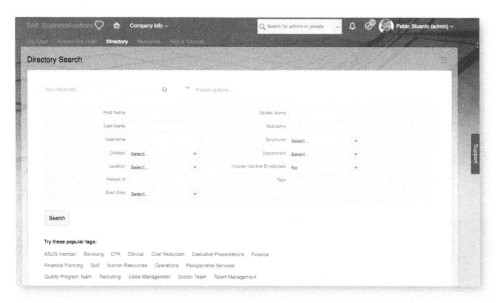

Figure 2.20: Company directory

Before we review how the search result looks, I want to make a point about tags.

Tags essentially allow people to associate people with different words. This can be an existing user of the system or even candidates applying to a job within Recruiting.

You may notice in Figure 2.20 at the bottom of the screen there are words, which represent the most popular tags in this particular system.

This becomes very handy if someone, for example, is looking to start a soccer team, or someone is looking for a CPA or a PMP. If you click on the actual word, anyone in the organization who has been "tagged" with that word will come up in the search results.

Once a search has been executed, Figure 2.21 shows search result screen.

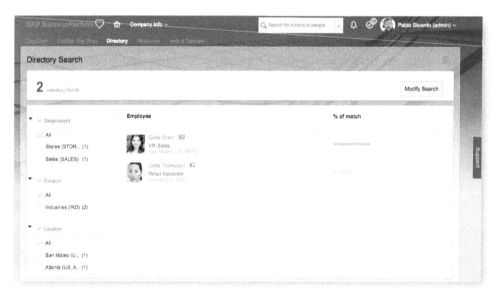

Figure 2.21: Directory search result screen

In the search result screen, users can see:

▶ The number of results found

▶ The actual people who the system found

▶ The % match for the results based on the criteria entered earlier

▶ Extra search fields

▶ The ability to modify the search

The company directory and org chart offer huge visibility for users and can be tools offering great help for a variety of reason; however, there is a third tool the system offers called resources. Let's see next what resources are all about.

Resources

Company resources is essentially a screen that allows administrators to technically put anything they want. In my experience I have seen companies put:

▶ General information about the system

▶ General information about the company

▶ Videos

▶ Images

▶ Instructions

As seen in Figure 2.22 for my system, I have designed a page with some introductory text and quick links to different resources.

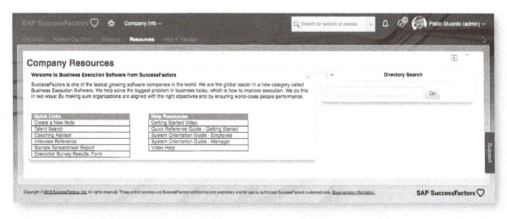

Figure 2.22: Company resources

49

As you might be noticing already, SuccessFactors offers a really cool and robust platform with all kind of features and functionality.

This is just the start. There is much more to be covered, including a very important item, Admin Center (OneAdmin), so let's see what this is all about.

2.2   Admin Center

Admin Center is the name of the side of SuccessFactors that controls the majority of the system configuration.

Admin Center is a screen that should only be accessible to the company's system administrators because of the huge power it has over all modules.

Next generation of Admin Center
In early 2016, SuccessFactors released the next generation of Admin Center. Administrators can use either screen, which offer the same functionality, with the main differences in the UI. In this book we will only use the legacy Admin Center, which is the most used one in the industry.

As you can see in Figure 2.23 Admin Center is a pretty complex screen with all sorts of information. Let's explore more about it.

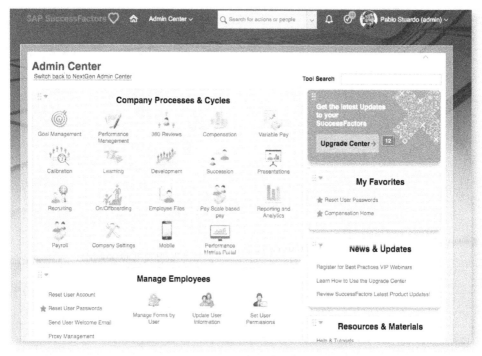

Figure 2.23: SuccessFactors Admin Center

2.2.1 Company processes & cycles

In this section of Admin Center, there are icons of all modules of SuccessFactors (regardless whether you have implemented them or not).

If someone clicks on an icon, a set of different configuration options will appear for each module. As an example, in Figure 2.24, I am hovering over Performance Management, and a menu with configuration options displays there.

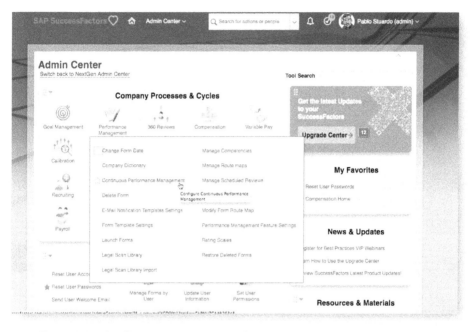

Figure 2.24: Configuration options in performance management icon

2.2.2 Manage employees

In this section an administrator can control general data about employees. Everything from reset passwords to proxy to update user information data like email, address, etc.

Also in this section the security structure of the system is controlled, which we are dedicating a whole chapter to it later in this book.

2.2.3 Upgrade Center

Upgrade Center allows users to perform certain upgrades to the system. If you remember back in chapter 1 when we discussed the different types of upgrades, for the Admin opt-in upgrades, Upgrade Center would be the place to perform the upgrades as shown in Figure 2.25.

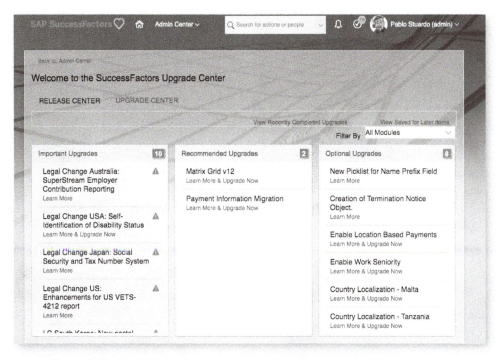

Figure 2.25: Upgrade Center

My favorites

In this section all the different links that have been marked as favorites will display for easy navigation.

New & updates

Administrators can find resources here, such as:

▶ SuccessFactors webinars

▶ Instructions on how to use the Upgrade Center

▶ Review the latest product updates

Resources & materials

In this section, administrators can find a variety of links including:

- ▶ Help & tutorial
- ▶ RBP access
- ▶ Access to the customer community
- ▶ Handout builder
- ▶ Refer SuccessFactors to people

There are other tools in the platform that can be accessed via Admin Center. Let's take a look at these tools now.

- ▶ Performance metric portal

This tool allows administrators to see data such as how many people have logged into the system at any point in time, or how much time users are spending on each module.

- ▶ Integration center

This allows administrators and consultants to easily integrate Success-Factors data with third-party system. This tool is very similar to a middleware.

- ▶ Release center

With this, administrator can see and understand exactly which universal updates will be applied to the system in the next quarterly release.

- ▶ Event center

This area allows users to see any event or workflow that might be associated with them. This is related to intelligence services.

Like mentioned earlier, Admin Center is an extremely powerful tool, in which the majority of configuration and governance of the system happens.

In this book 1 we will not necessarily cover everything related to Admin Center (which quite frankly would involve many books to even start describing everything that can be done here), but we will definitely touch upon a few items of Admin Center in later chapters.

The last section of this chapter covers the employee profile which is a critical piece of SuccessFactors. Let's learn more about it next.

2.3   Employee profile

Employee profile is a very important part of the system because it essentially stores all data related to the employee, including:

► Personal data

► Organizational data

► All data coming from each different module

Imagine having a folder with all data related to the employee, such as performance reviews, offer letters, compensation statements, etc. Employee profile is the same concept.

Although the term employee profile is accepted and used in the industry to describe this module of SuccessFactors, the true name of the tool that will be described next is people profile.

New version fo employee profile

The old version of employee profile was called employee profile and was divided into "profile" and "public profile". The new version is called "people profile". We will use people profile in this book because that is the new version and the most relevant one.

2.3.1 People profile

People profile stores all sorts of information about each employee. As seen in Figure 2.26, employee profile is composed of a rather large "header" which includes:

▶ Basic employee information such as title and work location

▶ Photo of the employee

▶ A short summary of the employee

▶ % of profile completion

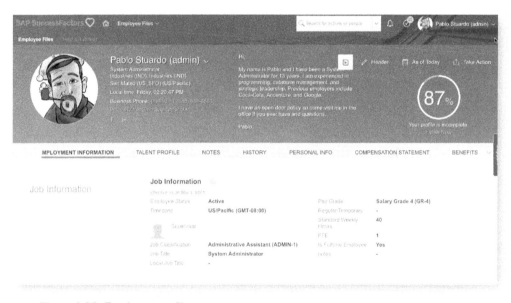

Figure 2.26: Employee profile

In addition to the header, the core of people profile are sections and blocks. Let's explore more about them.

56

Sections

Sections in employee profile are essentially groups of related data. For example, information related to:

- ▶ Employee information
- ▶ Previous work experience
- ▶ Education
- ▶ Skills

And much more would be grouped under the talent profile section. If we look back at Figure 2.26, you can see that sections will be listed next to each other right underneath the profile header. Once a user clicks on each section, the data below will be all related data.

Each section is built on blocks. Let's see what blocks are about.

Blocks

The idea of people profile is to store all employee data. However, this can be quite a bit of data; therefore, it is very important for the data to be well organized.

We already learned that data in people profile is grouped in sections. Each section contains blocks of fields that store data.

If we look at Figure 2.27, we can see that under the section employment information, we have a block called job information, and within this block we have different data fields storing job information such as:

- ▶ Employment status
- ▶ Time zone
- ▶ Manager
- ▶ Job classification
- ▶ Job title
- ▶ Pay grade
- ▶ Effective data

Figure 2.27: Sections and blocks in employee profile

Employee profile is very powerful because pretty much all modules can send information to people profile.

There are two very important concepts I really want to stress about people profile:

1. There is no limit to the number of sections, blocks and data fields that a system can have. Everything in people profile is configurable which means that administrators can add or remove fields, arrange items, change the name or text, etc.

    To try to illustrate the flexibility of the tool, I once had a huge client in the manufacturing industry. As an organization, they put a lot of emphasis on six sigma practices; therefore, we built a section called Six Sigma, and within the section we had blocks for relevant certifications, job experience, special projects, etc.

    In addition, people profile is 100% mobile responsive and pretty much everything you see in people profile can be reported.

2. There is a huge degree of granularity for security of people profile. Of course we would not want everyone to see anyone's salary information or performance reviews, or social security numbers. Therefore, the security for people profile goes to the data field level.

    We can define who gets to see what and who gets to edit what. For example, if we only want HR people to be able to see someone's SSN, we can define that. If we only want managers to be able to see performance review history for only their direct reports, we can define that.

    There are so many examples we could give, however the takeaway here is that SuccessFactors takes very seriously security, especially regarding who can see and edit data, which we will review in detail later in the book when we discuss security.

In summary, it would take many books to describe in detail everything related to the SuccessFactors platform and employee profile; however, the information just provided gives an excellent overview, and solid foundation to continue learning about SuccessFactors.

You will notice that after learning about each module, everything will start to make more sense because everything starts connecting with each other. In Chapter 3 you will learn all about career development.

3 Career development

As we have been looking into the employee cycle, it is time for each employee to set up their own development goals and/or partner with their manager to work on this.

The career development module, oftentimes called just development, is a very dynamic module that allows employees to not only track their development goals, but also lets them know exactly where they are and what they need to do to be ready to take other roles in the organization.

Let's explore more about the career development plan.

3.1   Career development plan

In SuccessFactors there are two types of goals:

► Performance goals (known as just "goals")

► Development goals

Performance goals are basically all goals that have direct impact into the core objectives of the organization. These are normally SMART goals (specific, measurable, attainable, relevant, time-bound), and are aligned between teams and cascaded from top leadership. An example can be: "Increase sales 20% by year end". These goals are tracked in the goals management module.

Development goals are associated with the employee himself and his/her overall development as an employee. These goals don't neces-sarily need to be time-bound, and even the measurable component can be a grey area.

For example, a development goal can be "Improve communication skills". If we think about it, this can be a rather subjective measure.

While keeping this in mind, the first component of the development mod-ule is the development plan itself, which looks almost exactly the same as a goal management plan as shown in Figure 3.1.

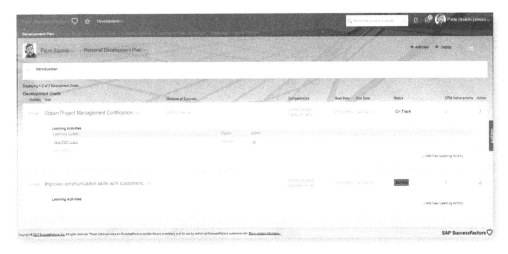

Figure 3.1: Development plan

If we look closely, on top we will have, just like in goals management, the option to toggle between development plans (Figure 3.2).

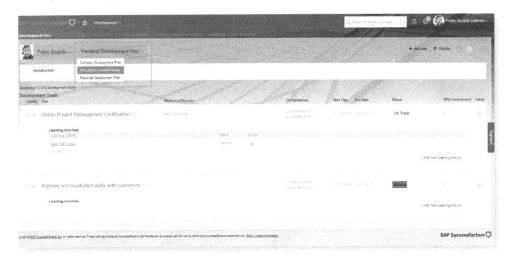

Figure 3.2: Different goal plans in development

Although in the example of Figure 3.2 there are two development plans plus a disciplinary incident history form, in my opinion it is always best to only have one development plan. This because, development goals should be constant and there should be continuous improvement, regardless of the time and circumstances.

Right below the different development plans, the actual development goal display. In a very same way as goals management, here you would create your own goals or have your manager create them.

Looking at Figure 3.3, we can see each goal:

Figure 3.3: Development goal details

▶ **Visibility**: It can be public or private. If it is private no one (not even your manager) can see the goals. If public, all the roles configured to see your development goals would display.

▶ **Goal Name**: This is just the name of the development goal.

▶ **Measure of Success**: What will mark the development goal as attained. Again, development goals can be sort like a grey area to quantify.

▶ **Competencies**: Any competencies attached to the development goal.

▶ **Start Date**: The start of the development goal.

▶ **Due date**: The due date in case there is one.

▶ **Status**: The color-based status of the development goal.

▶ **CPM Achievements**: These are any achievements coming from continuous performance that might be attached to this development goal.

In addition, there is the opportunity to perform an additional set of actions (Figure 3.4) including:

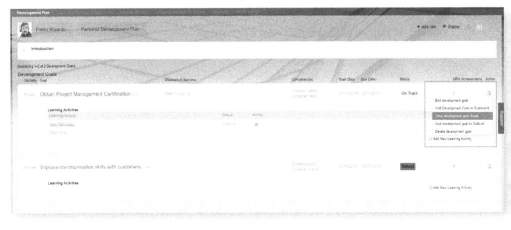

Figure 3.4: Additional actions for development goals

▶ **Edit the development goal**: Here the user would have the opportunity to edit the data we discussed earlier, such as name, measure of success, status, etc.

▶ **Add development goal in scorecard**: If you remember back in Chapter 2 with employee profile, there are many portlets or blocks of data relevant for each module. One of the blocks that contains data from different modules such as succession, development, performance, etc. is the employee scorecard. This option allows to publish the development goal in the block or portlet of the scorecard.

▶ **View goal details**: This option, in a very similar way to goals management, allows to see audit information about the development goal; when was it created and by whom, who has edited information about the goal, etc.

▶ **Add development goal to outlook**: This option will allow you to create an appointment in Outlook (or any other email service provider) to performance activities related to the goal. In the example of Figure 3.4, I have a goal to "Obtain project management certification", so with this option I could click it, and create an appointment with myself every Monday to study 1 hour in the mornings.

▶ **Delete development goal**: This is self-explanatory. This option would remove the goal from the development goal plan permanently.

Also, probably you have already noticed that on each goal, there is a little link that says "Add New Learning Activity" (Figure 3.5).

Figure 3.5: Add learning activity to development goal.

This option allows the user to add a learning activity to be attached to the goal. There are two options available here:

1. **Find from catalog**: This is the direct integration with the learning module. It would look at your current job code and/or role, and see if in the learning section there are activities or training available for particular competencies associated with job codes and/or roles.

2. **Custom learning activities**: This option allows you to create a manual learning activity. If we look at Figure 3.6 we can see how the wizard works and how it allows the user to enter anything with no restrictions.

Figure 3.6: Adding a new learning activity to a development goal

65

Now that we have a good understanding of how to track development goals, let learn more about the career worksheet.

3.2   Career worksheet

There is truly no point at developing and spending time performing different learning activities unless we have a clear path to where we want to go.

If you think about it, the majority of people have a job in which it seems like the only way to move up the organization is by moving to other companies, which has a huge negative impact (retention).

What the career worksheet tool tries to solve is to offer information about exactly:

▶   Where you stand in your current role

▶   What your career path is like

▶   What do you need to do or focus on to get there

Let's review a bit more about these functions.

In Figure 3.7, we can see that there is a squared-shaped box with my current role.

Let's imagine this is a real scenario. You could come here and obviously see what your current role is, and how long you have had this role.

In addition, if we scroll down, we will be able to see all the competencies associated with that job role (Figure 3.8).

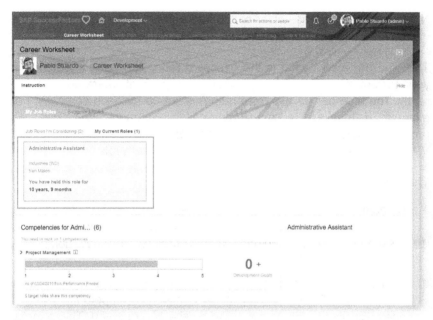

Figure 3.7: Career worksheet current role view

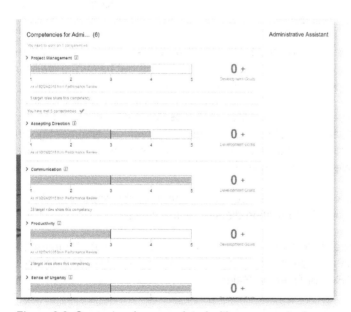

Figure 3.8: Competencies associated with my current role.

Notice that each bar has color-coded bar, with a 1–5 number that are the value of a rating scale we have configured in the system.

The blue bar marks what is the expected rating for that competency in your current role. The yellow-greenish bar represent where are you currently. The blue bar (or expected rating) is set up for each company. For example, if there was a competency called "communication skills", we probably would have an expected rating of 100% (the maximum) for a VP of sales role, but a rating of 75% for a sales intern role.

There are two ways to get this updated:

1. By having a performance review. Career worksheet would grab the ratings for the latest performance review that was completed for you (assuming your performance review process includes competencies).

2. By launching a role readiness assessment form which is similar to a performance form, but only covers relevant competencies and it goes directly to your manager, so he/she can rate you. These forms can be launched at any time, and as many times as you want, so you don't have to wait a whole performance cycle to get some type of formal assessment.

Let's pause for a second and think. Okay, we understand where we are and we have a tool to evaluate our current role without having to wait for a formal review process, but what else. What's the whole point of this?

Well, as discussed earlier, the whole purpose of development is to offer tools for individuals that not only allows them to track development goals and learning activities, but also let them know exactly where they are and how to move up in the hierarchy.

If we take a look at Figure 3.9, we can see that for the same employee, now a different set of information display on the screen.

Career worksheet allows users to search for jobs they might be interested on. In this case I defined that I am considering the roles of "IT Project Manager" and "Senior Director, Sales".

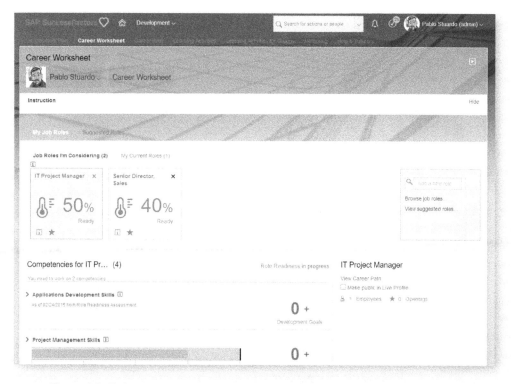

Figure 3.9: Roles I am considering in career worksheet.

You will notice that in the top (Figure 3.9) there are two thermometers. These thermometers are letting me know what percentage of "readiness" I have to be ready to take on the role.

This is calculated by the expected rating for the needed competencies for the role vs my current ratings.

So let's pause for a second. Imagine your current role. Now imagine you had a tool that allowed you to search for other potential opportunities within the company, and a tool that would tell you exactly which competencies you need to work on in order to be qualified for the role.

It doesn't stop there. If we look at Figure 3.10 we can even add development goals for each competencies (of the role we are considering) in efforts to accelerate the readiness process.

Figure 3.10: Add development goals for competencies in career worksheet

If someone is ready to get re-assessed by his/her manager, the person would simply click on role readiness assessment and launch the form as shown in Figure 3.11 and Figure 3.12.

Figure 3.11: Launch role readiness assessment

Figure 3.12: Roles readiness assessment

Now let's take this to even a deeper level.

If you notice (in Figure 3.10) to the right of the screen there is more information (Figure 3.13).

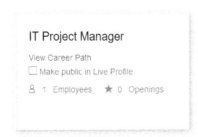

Figure 3.13: Additional actions in career worksheet

At the top you see the name of the role you are considering, but not only that. If we click on "View career path" you can understand exactly where this potential role would take you as shown in Figure 3.14.

As you can see, clearly we know that an IT Analyst has the opportunity to decide to go for Information Systems Manager or IT Manager.

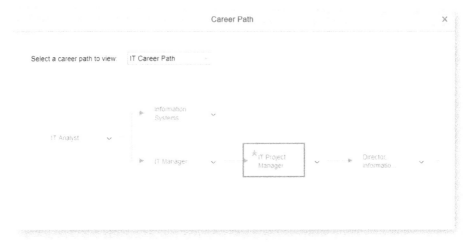

Figure 3.14: Career path within career worksheet

If the IT Manager route was taken the next role up would be IT Project Manager and then next one up Director or Information System.

Not only that, but if we click on any of this roles, even more relevant information about the role would appear.

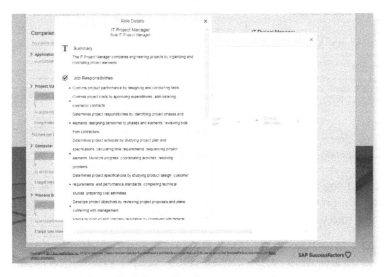

Figure 3.15: Job profile information from career path

With SuccessFactors development, we not only get a very graphical and interactive career path, but it also shows everything that makes up the career path is connected and fed by other modules.

Now this is an extremely powerful concept if you think about it.

At this point we have a tool that:

- ▶ Allows us to understand where we are in the organization
- ▶ Allows us to see where we would like to go by looking at job descriptions and career paths
  Allows us to select roles we are considering and
  - ▶ See exactly in which areas (competencies) we need to focus on
  - ▶ Add development goals to those competencies
  - ▶ Add learning activities, whether integrated with the learning module or our own learning activities to achieve those goals
- ▶ Doesn't have to wait a whole performance cycle to get a formal assessment on your competencies

Now what else could you need? This seems to offer all relevant information to see where you stand and how to get to your next level within the company.

Well not so fast. The last piece of the puzzle is to actually move into that role.

Imagine you have a role you are considering, and you have worked very hard to have all the qualifications for the role and your manager is in full alignment and agreement with your aspirations.

If we look at Figure 3.16 the system will tell you who is already in that particular role you are considering, and lets you navigate to their contact information in case you have questions or would simply like to contact the person, really making a statement and enhancing company collaboration.

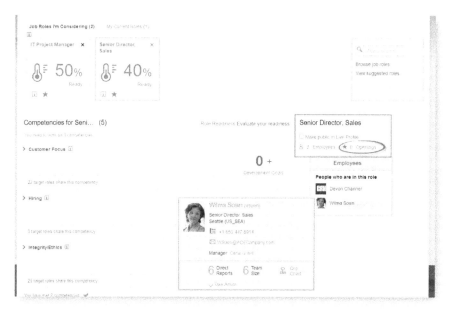

Figure 3.16: Others in the role and job openings

In addition, the system will tell you if there are any job openings for that particular role! All data coming from recruiting management, and of course you can directly apply if there were any positions open for the role.

Now this is pretty cool and exciting functionality. You basically have everything you need to be able to know how to move up in the organization.

Now that we know about the two core features of the development module (development plan and career worksheet), let's learn a bit more about learning activities.

3.3   Learning activities

Another smaller, but very useful function that the development module offers is learning activities" (Figure 3.17).

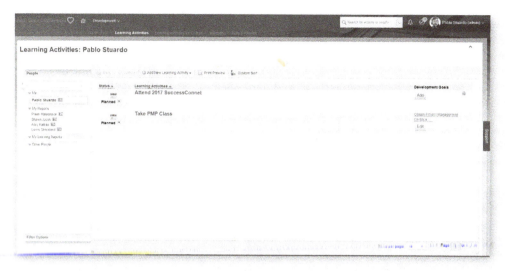

Figure 3.17: Learning activities within development

This learning activity management system basically groups all learning activities relevant for you, whether these were added to each development goal or shared as a group.

In this screen you can not only see all learning activities associated with you, but also you can mark them as completed, and even print them as shown in Figure 3.18.

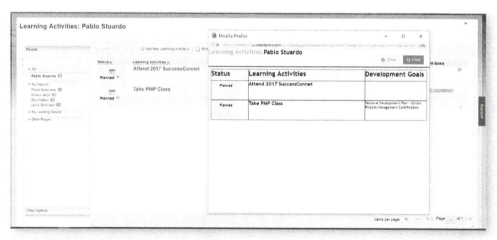

Figure 3.18: Print learning activities within development

75

Within learning activities, with the right authorization, you can also see your team's learning activities.

Earlier we mentioned that learning activities could be taking from the development plan, which was added to each development goal, and also shared by groups.

That's an extra feature offered in the system. Let's say we would like to add a learning activity for attending a professional conference to all members of a service line.

We could easily create a group for all those individuals (Figure 3.19).

Figure 3.19: Learning activities group

And mass assign learning activities to the entire group (Figure 3.20).

With learning activities we finalize our introduction to career development.

76

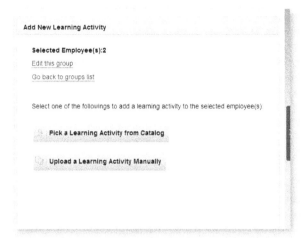

Figure 3.20: Mass assign learning activities to learning groups

You should really understand not only how powerful this module is, but also how powerful, dynamic and connected the entire SuccessFactors suite is designed.

This module allows users to understand exactly where they stand in the organization, and what they need to focus on to move into the roles they might consider in the future.

All this by also providing the necessary tools to track and keep consistent the employee development process while connecting with other modules to produce an even stronger synergy.

Now let's learn about goals management next.

4 Goals management

Goals management allows employees and managers to track and align performance goals and company-wide objectives.

"Goals" and "objectives"

The words "goals" and "objectives" in SuccessFactors will mean the same in this book, just like in the industry.

The whole purpose is to offer users a tool to track goals to ensure people are working on things that truly matter. Goals management has cross integration points with:

- ▶ Performance management
  - ▶ Display goals in performance forms
  - ▶ Continuous performance
- ▶ Onboarding
  - ▶ Pre-day 1 hire experience which allows new hires to start tracking goals or review them even before day 1
- ▶ Employee profile
  - ▶ Data from goals can be stored in the employee profile

Let's begin reviewing the main features and capabilities by learning about the goals template.

4.1 Goals template

A goals template is the backbone of the module. Essentially it is a screen in which users can see all the goals associated with a particular goal plan in a very similar fashion as development goals.

Let's look at Figure 4.1 and see what makes up this goal plan.

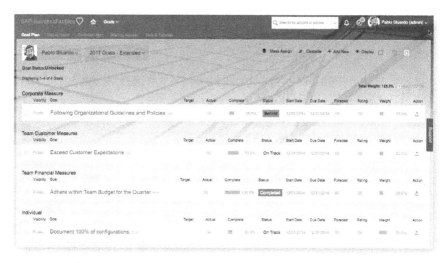

Figure 4.1: Goal template

At the very top, you see an image and name of either yourself or an employee.

The default is to see yourself and your own goals, however, let's say you would like to review how one of your direct reports is doing, you could simply click on the name and search for an employee as shown in Figure 4.2.

Figure 4.2: Search for other's goal plan

Of course, like everything else in SuccessFactors, security is extremely important, so every user has to have the correct permissions for what they can see or do with goal plans.

Most likely you will be able to see your own goal plan, and see and edit your direct reports.

Right next to the employee name you will see another drop-down menu with the current goal plan as shown in Figure 4.3.

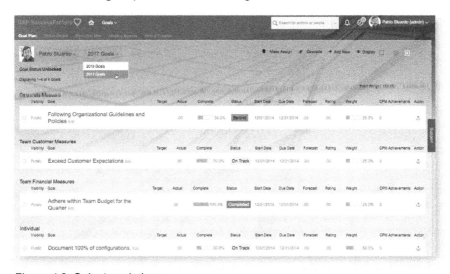

Figure 4.3: Select goal plans

The options in this case are two goal plans:

▶ 2016 Goals

▶ 2017 Goals

These are all the goal plans available to this particular individual. Normally organizations will have one goal plan per year; however, in my experience I have seen goal plans per quarter (for one part of the population), or also different goal plans based on different criteria, such as a financial or management goal plan, etc.

It is up to the organization to decide the strategy for the number of goal plans; however, each goal plan can be configured to look a bit different and be able to perform better reporting cycle after cycle.

Let's continue analyzing what is available in a goal plan.

4.1.1 Categories

Looking at Figure 4.4, we can see goals listed under four categories:

- ▶ Corporate measure
- ▶ Team customer measures
- ▶ Team financial measures
- ▶ Individual

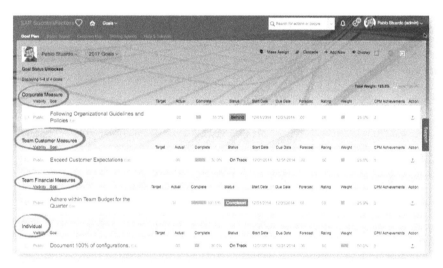

Figure 4.4: Goals categories

Categories are configurable at the goal template level, which means that we can add, remove, or change the name of each category for each of our goal plans. Categories are used to group different goals.

Goals

Under each category, we are able to see goals since the whole point is to track goals, which are made up of:

▶ Goal name

▶ Goal description

▶ Target

▶ Actual

▶ % completion

▶ Status

▶ Dates

▶ Weights

▶ Achievements (cross integration with continuous performance).

The items listed above make sense. We need to be identify what will be tracked, and then offered different data fields to maintain the tracking such as goal status.

These fields are standard, and in many cases can be considered best practices. The goal template itself is flexible enough to allow each organization to shape the plan however they want to add or remove fields to track goal information.

SMART goal wizard

There is a lot of research about what is a goal, and SuccessFactors offers best practice tools in the industry to add goals that take the approach of the SMART goal concept, specifically:

▶ Specific

▶ Measurable

▶ Attainable

▶ Relevant

▶ Time-bound

Let's take a look at Figure 4.5.

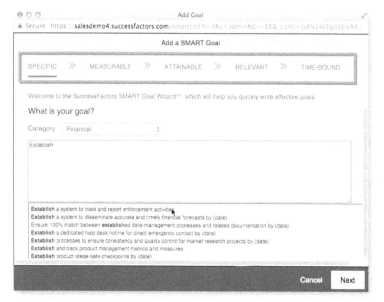

Figure 4.5: Specific, SMART goal wizard

Here we can see how the SMART goal wizard looks. On top it has the five elements, and it takes the user through each one while defining and creating goals by asking the right questions.

In the next four images we can clearly see how useful this tool can become for managers to create goals in the right language.

Uploading goal libraries

 Goal libraries can be uploaded into the system in such a way that when someone is creating a goal, they would begin typing a word or a phrase, and the system can read the library and complete goal automatically as shown in Figure 4.5.

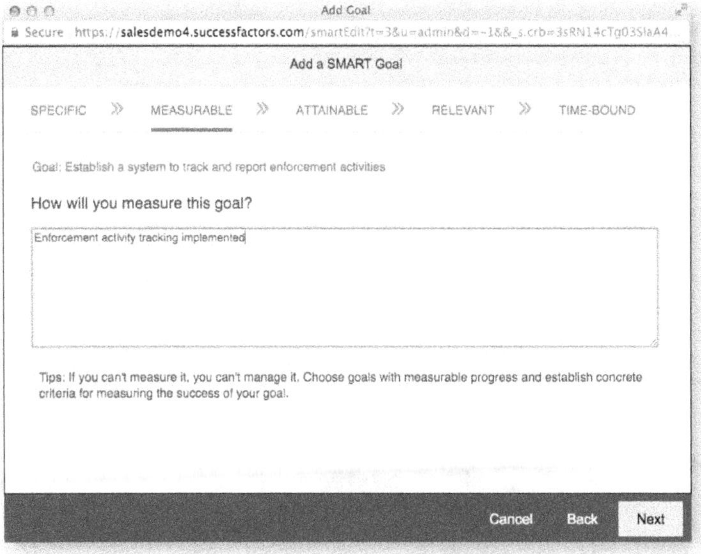

Figure 4.6: Measurable, SMART goal wizard

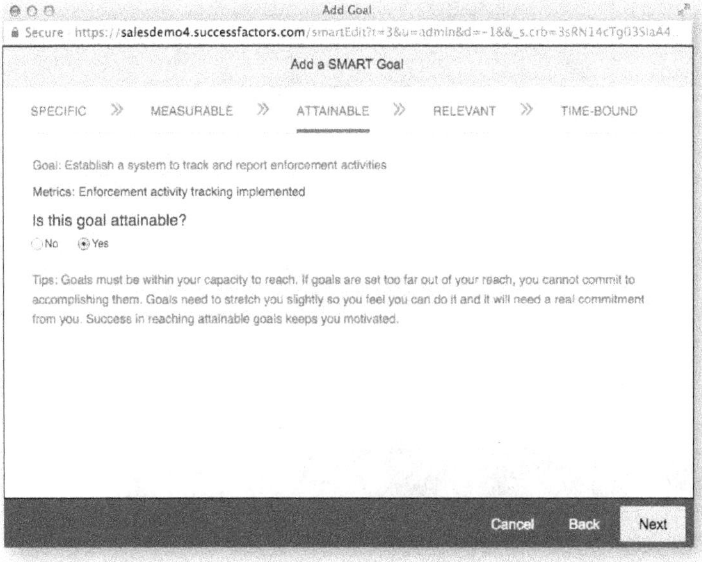

Figure 4.7: Attainable, SMART goal wizard

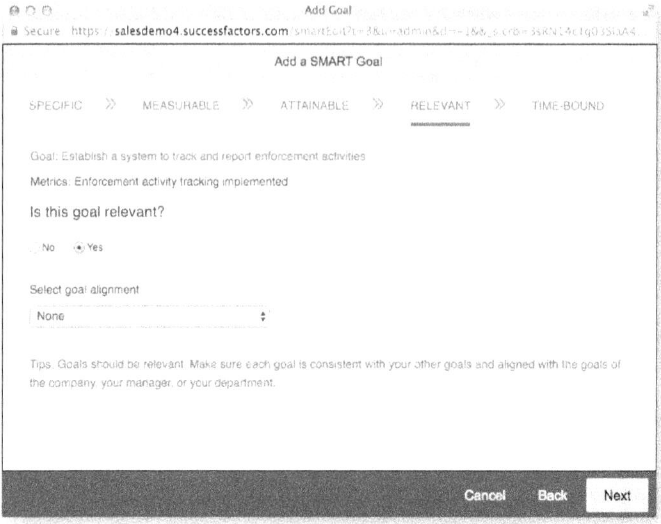

Figure 4.8: Relevant, SMART goal wizard

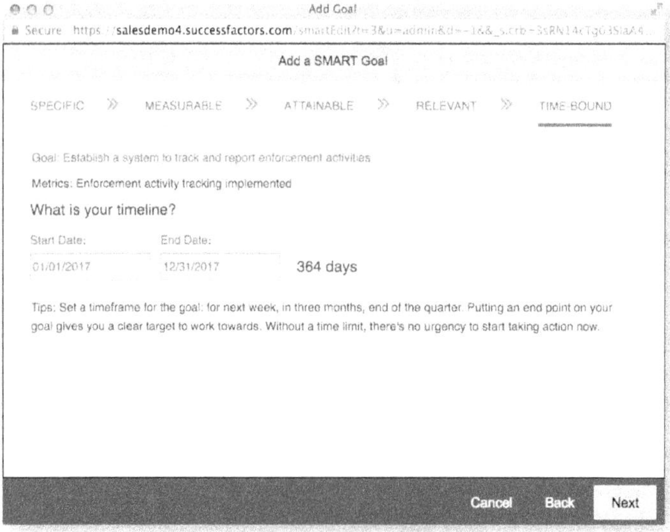

Figure 4.9: Time-bound, SMART goal wizard

4.1.2 Cascading goals

It is simply not possible to stay competitive in today's world if individuals work on goals that don't align somehow with the overall organization's strategy.

Goals management allows individual to cascade goals and share goals between employees and teams.

When we look at Figure 4.10, we can see an image that showcases the process to cascade goals.

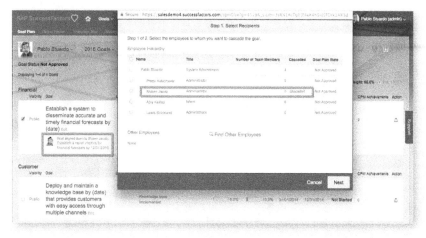

Figure 4.10: Cascade goals down to a direct report

We can see that Pablo Stuardo, System Administrator, cascaded a goal with Shawn Jacob.

There can be an approval process in order to align (cascade) goals up or down the organization.

4.2 Other actions

There are other actions that can be done with goals. Let's explore those.

4.2.1 Edit goals

Once a goal has been created, individuals need to track them by changing the status and any extra information that might be required. Figure
4.11 displays an image on how this would be achieved.

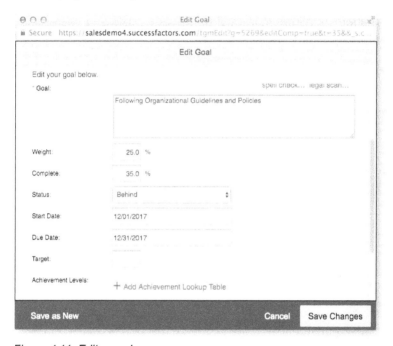

Figure 4.11: Edit a goal

4.2.2 View goal details

In addition, especially for admins, there can be an option to view goal
details, which in addition to be able to see overall information about the
goal (Figure 4.12), users can also see the audit history of the goal.

Figure 4.12: View goal details

4.2.3 Goal alignment spotlight

Users also can have the ability to see a report on the alignment of a particular goal.

Figure 4.13 shows an image of how this would look.

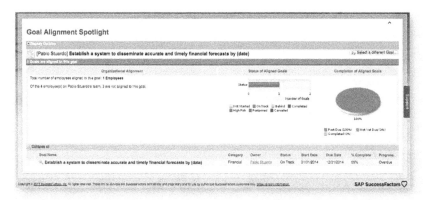

Figure 4.13: Goal alignment spotlight

4.3 Goal execution

In addition to the actions just introduced, there is another side called goals execution, which is composed by three features:

▶ Status report

▶ Execution map

▶ Meeting agenda

Let's see what these are all about.

4.3.1 Status report

Status report, as shown in Figure 4.14, allow users to send reports about goals to a manager.

Figure 4.14: Status report

In the status report, users will see the different goals associated with a particular goal plan, in addition to other metrics such as:

▶ Execution actual

▶ Execution target

▶ Level of effort

▶ Probability of success

▶ Comments

Users will fill out the required information and then send it to their manager. A manager will receive a notification about it.

4.3.2 Execution map

Execution map allows users to visually see what the team (or overall organization is working on). If we look at Figure 4.15, we can see how goals that have been aligned (cascaded) are represented visually.

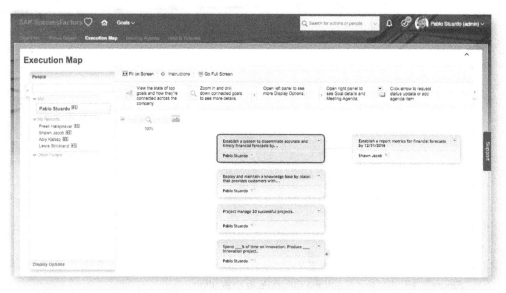

Figure 4.15: Execution Map

In this case I am looking at myself (my own goals), and I can see where those have been aligned to.

With the right authorization, users can look at different people's goals and dynamically navigate to the cascading relationships.

Not only that, but within each goal presented in the screen, users can take additional actions such as (Figure 4.16):

▶ Ask goal owner for a status update

▶ Add this goal to meeting agenda watch list

▶ Remove this goal from meeting agenda watch list

▶ Save goal as JPEG

▶ Save goal as PDF

▶ Print this goal (Figure 4.17 shows an image of how this would look in PDF format)

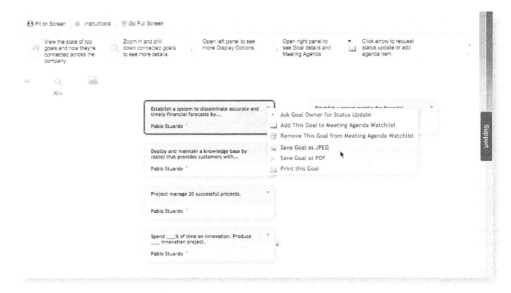

Figure 4.16: Additional actions for goals in execution map

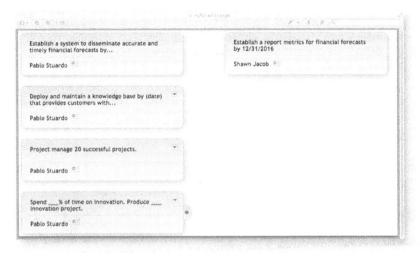

Figure 4.17: Execution map goals printed in PDF format

4.3.3   Meeting agenda

Meeting agenda is probably one of my favorite features out of goal execution. This feature is designed for managers to have goal information that can be easily used to conduct a meeting with a team.

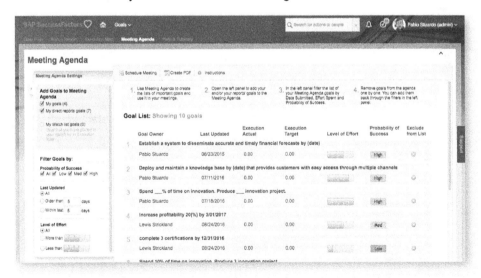

Figure 4.18: Meeting agenda

In Figure 4.18 we can see how a manager could select goals utilizing different filters (on the left), with information coming directly from the status report.

The goals selected would display in the center of the screen. Imagine if you would like to have a meeting with your team about all goals that have a low probability of success, and come up with a team strategy to achieve those.

With this tool, you can clearly identify those, select them and then create a PDF with those as shown in Figure 4.19.

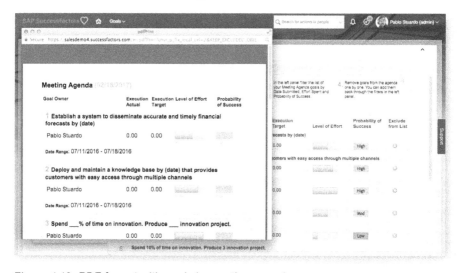

Figure 4.19: PDF format with goals in meeting agenda

This PDF document would only include goals that were selected after utilizing the filters. These filters include:

- ▶ My goals
- ▶ My direct report goals
- ▶ Watch list goals (from execution map)
- ▶ Probability of success
- ▶ Last updated
- ▶ Level of effort

This PDF document can be used as a handout to share with the team.

Also, meeting agenda includes a feature to softly integrate with an email provider. After goals have been selected by the click of one button, a manager can create an .ics file, which is the format to add meetings into MS Outlook, Google Calendar, Apple Calendar, etc.

The cool part is that once the meeting invitation has being created and sent to the rest of the team, the system will automatically attach to the invitation the same PDF document generated earlier as shown in Figure 4.20 (in this case I am using an Apple device, but this functionality is compatible across all major email providers).

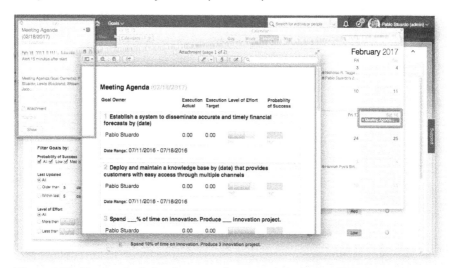

Figure 4.20: Meeting invitation from meeting agenda including PDF document with goals data

In summary, this module is one of the oldest and most popular of the entire SuccessFactors suite; it allows users to not only track goals in different goal plans, but it also offers very dynamic tools to ensure people are working on the right things which also align with the overall objective of the company.

Let's see how goals can impact the actual performance of an individual by learning more about performance management next.

5 Performance management

By now you should have a clear understanding of the overall platform in addition to some of the HR business functions SuccessFactors offers.

We have already explored the platform and employee profile, and started the journey into alignment and performance with the introduction of goals management and career development.

In this chapter we continue exploring the whole concept of alignment and performance with the introduction of performance management.

Performance management is my personal favorite, and in my opinion the most mature module in the SuccessFactors suite.

If we remember from chapter 1, SuccessFactors started as a cloud solution for performance and then it quickly evolved into the incredible tool it is today.

Performance management offers companies an entire suite to maintain your performance reviews for the entire employee population, but it also allows constant conversation tracking and feedback with the inclusion of continuous performance. SuccessFactors performance management also integrates with other modules.

Let's learn more about this exciting module.

5.1.1 Performance management process

Before we dive too quickly into performance forms, let's review the actual process that is provided.

The best way to understand performance forms is to imagine a Word document or sheet of paper. In the context of performance, remember the last performance review you had. Most likely it was done on a MS Word document.

The form probably had a standardized structure with header, section for comments, rating, etc. Now imagine this exact same concept of a form, but with the flexibility to modify it however you want, in addition to very cool and useful functionality for a better user experience.

In a nutshell that is what a performance form is all about. mimicking what otherwise would have been a paper form or a form done in a Microsoft Office product (Word—Excel) in one system shared by everyone with extra functionality and cross integration opportunities with other modules (processes).

Now that we have an understanding of a performance form, of which we will learn more in detail later in this chapter, let's discuss the performance process.

SuccessFactors performance

 SuccessFactors performance is incredible flexible and can accommodate many processes that would take a whole book to explain. Therefore, in this book we are basing the discussion on best practices and my experience with best real company use cases.

SuccessFactors has a tool called route maps, which are essentially workflows that can be attached to forms and control how they move from one user to another.

As shown in Figure 5.1, route maps are constructed by steps in a process (or a workflow), which in this case defines that this performance form should have:

1. Employee self-assessment
2. Manager evaluation
3. 1:1 meeting
4. Signature of the manager
5. Completion of the form

in chronological order.

Figure 5.1: Route map Example

Route maps can be fully customized, which means that you can have as many or few steps in the process as you want. In addition, admins can control:

▶ The text for each step

▶ The user role (manager, employee, 2nd level manager, etc.) that should complete the step

▶ Any description associated with the step

▶ Translations for text in the step

Therefore, the first task in any performance management process is to understand the performance process itself for each organization. This will probably change from company to company, but for this chapter we will stick to the example in Figure 5.1.

Once we have our route map defined and configured with our performance template, which we will discuss in the next section, the next step in the overall process is launching a performance form to all employees that should get one by an administrator with the click of a button.

For example, let's say we have developed a performance template for all salaried employees. An admin would go to the launch option in Admin Center, select the template, define the user population who should receive the form (all salaried employees), and launch the forms.

By doing the steps above the system will make a copy from the template which is the blueprint of the structure of the form, and create one per employee; so imagine if your organization has 50,000 employees, with the click of one button, all of them will get an individual performance form. This form will then move in the process based on the route map defined previously.

Now that we have a solid understanding of what a performance form is, the concept of route maps, and the overall process of launching forms, let's learn more about performance templates, which are the basis of each performance form.

5.1.2   Performance templates

We can define templates as the place in which the structure and configuration of each form will be defined based on sections and different features.

Before we start learning more about them, in order to explain each template, the images you will see are from an actual performance form.

Let's review the types of sections available:

Section types

There are many section types within a performance template. SuccessFactors performance is flexible enough to allow the use of only the sections you need to support your current process.

For example, imagine that a company only does performance evaluations based on performance and development goals, but they don't use competencies, well then they would not see the competency section.

Let's review each section:

▶   Form name and pods

The first section on any performance template is the form name and pods as shown in Figure 5.2.

Figure 5.2: Form name and pods

Notice that the text at the very top is the name of the performance form. This name can be modified to say anything culturally the company uses such as:

▶ Performance review

▶ Performance evaluation

▶ Performance appraisal

Then, the very next section is a photo of the employee or subject, which is the person being reviewed. Right next to it, there are 5 available pods. Let's review what pods are and what they can do.

▶ Overall score pod:

The overall score pod shown in Figure 5.3 displays information about the overall rating of the form. This pod directly grabs the information from the overall score section at the bottom of the form, which can be based only on competencies (most common way) or can be a combination of competencies and goal ratings.

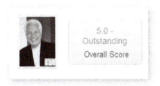

Figure 5.3: Overall score pod

When the user clicks on the pod, a new window will be displayed showing details of what has been rated.

101

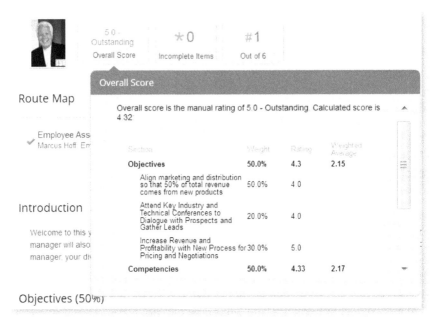

Figure 5.4: Overall score pod expanded

▶ Incomplete items pod:

The incomplete items pod shown in Figure 5.5 displays information about all the items that are incomplete in the form which are required. If the configuration set that all competencies must be rated before moving to the next step in the process, this pod will display all the competencies that have not been rated yet.

Figure 5.5: Incomplete items pods

▶ Team rank pod:

The team rank pod in Figure 5.6 displays a ranking of the reviewer's direct reports based on overall ranking. This information (ranking) is limited to the same performance form. It does not mix ratings from other forms.

Figure 5.6: Team rank pod

If a form has not be completed yet, the pod will show a value of N/A for that particular direct report and will place him on the bottom of the ranking (Figure 5.7).

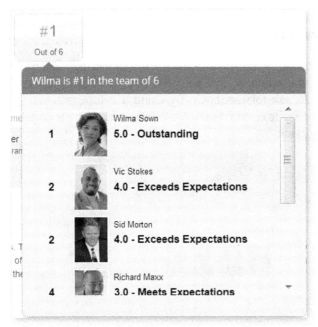

Figure 5.7: Team rank pod expanded

▶ Supporting information pod:

The supporting information pod in Figure 5.8 needs to be combined with the team overview functionality of the form for better use, and display information from other's feedback in addition to any notes that someone might have placed about the employee.

103

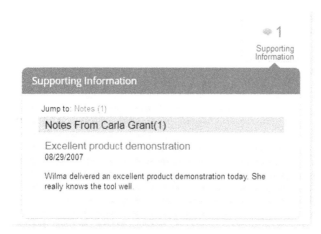

Figure 5.8: Supporting information pod

A new window will pop up as shown in Figure 5.9 and the user will have to click on the employee again. At this point the reviewer can select one or many employees to ask for feedback. By using this tool, you will be sending an email (using text has been pre-configured), which can be edited asking for feedback.

Figure 5.9: Ask for feedback

All the feedback provided will be displayed in the pod as supporting information once the user clicks on it.

▶ Gap analysis pod:

The gap analysis pod in Figure 5.10 displays information about the gap between self-assessment ratings and ratings given by the performance reviewer.

There must be a self-assessment step in the route map in order for this pod to work properly. Once the manager clicks on the pod, it will display a window with information about the gap between employee and manager rating. (Figure 5.11)

Figure 5.10: Gap analysis pod

Gap Analysis				
2 items rated higher than Wilma			3 items rated lower than Wilma	
Competencies	Gap		Competencies	Gap
Communication	+1.0		Customer Focus	-1.0
Objectives	Gap		Hiring	-1.0
Ensure rapid introduction and dist...	+1.0		Objectives	Gap
			Increase customer net promoter s...	-1.0

Figure 5.11: Gap analysis pod expanded

All these pods are independently managed; therefore, there is no need to have all of them enabled. Based on current practices there might be situations in which only one pod is required, and others in which two or more are required.

Also, there might be situations in which only managers can see the pods in the route map or only second-level managers. All these permissions and enablement of pods can be configured to meet customer needs.

Now that we have a good understanding of pods and the header of per-formance forms, let's continue learning more about the other sections available in a performance form.

▶ Instructions section

After a user sees (on top of the screen) the performance form name and all pods available, the next logical section is the instructions section.

Just like the name mentions it, this section is designed to offer users information about how to complete the form as shown in Figure 5.12.

Figure 5.12: Instruction section

When configuring the form template, the admin has the opportunity to modify this text. This is a text area field and it also supports some limited HTML in case someone would like to add images or hyperlinks.

▶ Goals/objective section

The next logical section in this form is the goals/objective section. If you remember, we use the goals module to track performance goals, which normally would be set at the beginning of the performance cycle.

In this organization example, we have determined that goals is a key component of the annual performance review and so we added them to our form.

Any goal we have added (in the goals module) to a pre-defined goal plan template will display in this section as shown in Figure 5.13.

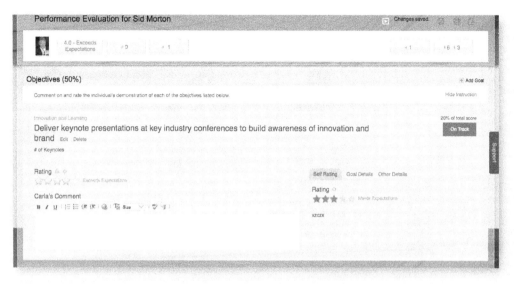

Figure 5.13: Goals management section

Notice that the reviewer, in addition to seeing information about the goal, can add a rating, which can be configured to be weighted for the overall performance score.

There is the opportunity to add a comments (as a manager), in addition to seeing the employee self-rating for the goal.

Performance forms are very flexible, so the fact you see a rating in this example, it doesn't mean you have to always rate items. There are many organizations that like to only display goal information in the performance forms, and comments or ratings are not needed.

In this case, the user can add other goals that will be dynamically added back to the goal plan in the goals module, but you can choose not to do so.

Having a goals section in performance is not required. Each organization chooses to display it there or not.

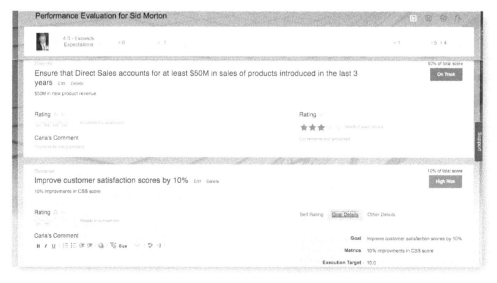

Figure 5.14: Goals section in performance form

In Figure 5.14, there is another image about how goals might look in a performance form.

After a user has seen all information relevant to the subject's goals, logi-cally it makes sense to review all competencies attached to each per-formance form.

▶ Competency section

Competencies can be defined as a set of behavior and descriptions that allow identifying and evaluating behaviors in individual employees. Some very common competencies can be:

▶ Communication

▶ Customer focus

▶ Business acumen

There can be literally hundreds of different competencies, and it all really depends on each organization.

I have seen organizations that only uses five core competencies across the entire organization for all employees, and I have seen companies that have a set of competencies based on each job code; and of course everything in between.

SuccessFactors can accommodate many competency libraries, allowing administrators to create custom competencies and map them to job codes and roles as needed. The system is extremely flexible with competencies and all of these can be translated.

In a very similar way to goals, competencies can be rated, and a comment can be provided as shown in Figure 5.15.

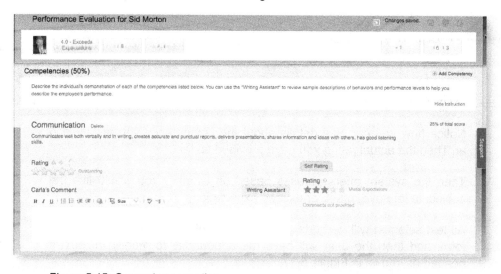

Figure 5.15: Competency section

A very nice functionality offered for the comment box is the Writing Assistant, which is a tool that allows users to provide better and more consistent comments during the process.

Imagine you are a manager, and you are evaluating a direct report. The direct report is not really performing well in a competency, but you are unsure how to structure your comments about it. If you were to use writing assistant as shown in Figure 5.16, the system would provide you with lists of potential text that could be used.

Figure 5.16: Writing assistant

Notice how you can see details about the competency you are looking at. Then the actual rating you have provided so far.

Then the system offers phrases based on whether you would like the subject to improve, meet, or exceed expectations.

All text selected will be added to the comments box in the performance form, and then the user will have the opportunity to modify the text if needed as shown in Figure 5.17.

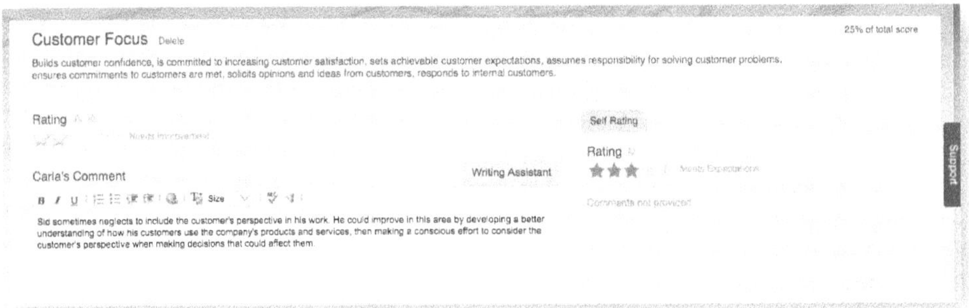

Figure 5.17: Text from writing assistant

▶ Development section

In a very same fashion as the goal section, the next logical section would be the development section, which displays all development goals being tracked as in Figure 5.18.

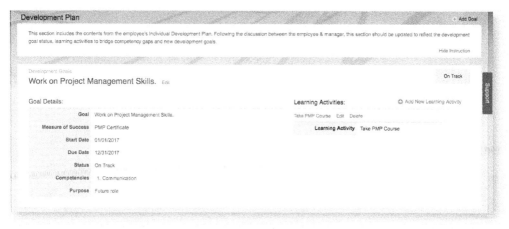

Figure 5.18: Development section

This section behaves pretty much just like the goals section.

At this point in the form, the user had the opportunity to review all necessary information to be able to make an educated decision about the overall rating of the subject.

Let's review the summary section.

▶ Summary section

The summary section is all about final ratings. There are essentially two possibilities here. You can have a calculated overall rating based on ratings and weights from items reviewed in earlier sections. Also there is a manual rating that allows the user to provide a final overall rating regardless of individual item ratings in earlier section.

The most common configuration is to actually have both calculated and manual rating as shown in Figure 5.19.

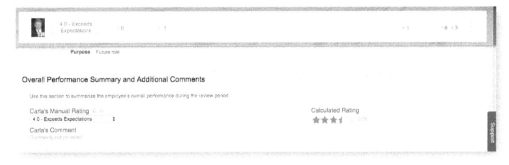

Figure 5.19: Summary section

Whichever rating is used, there must always be a final overall rating in order to integrate with other modules.

Technically you don't have to have a rating; you can have a performance form that only contains comments, however, you will miss a lot of functionality available in the system.

▶   Signature section

The last section in a performance form is the signature section. This section ideally would only appear at the very end of the process, and allows the parties involved in the process to electronically sign the form.

Figure 5.20: Signature section

Remember that all forms will be stored in the system for all users in all cycles. This becomes very handy for historical data, reporting and for any reason someone might need to see this information.

Performance forms are very flexible and can be adjusted to match your process and company culture. In addition, the overall functionality can be used in other creative ways. For example, I have created forms for:

- ▶ Disciplinary incident forms
- ▶ Salary increase request
- ▶ Vacation requests
- ▶ Surveys

The examples you saw earlier are only a handful of the dozens of different combinations that can be created to build the form that fits your organization.

Now that we have a better understanding of performance forms, let's discuss continuous performance.

5.1.3 Continuous performance

Continuous performance is a feature that allows companies, in addition to the concept of once or twice yearly performance evaluations, to have a tool that can offer constant communication and feedback between managers and direct reports.

Continuous performance allows managers to monitor and ensure employees are working on the right items at the right time, and allows employees to provide feedback to their managers on the tasks, contributions, and achievements they might be involved in.

Some key features of continuous performance include:

Tracking—Tasks and activities employees are involved.

Structure—Lists of all activities, tasks, achievements, etc. are available at all times to use as a base for one-on-one discussions at any time.

Goal plan—There is a direct integration with goals and development so all activities available in continuous performance can be integrated to ensure that alignment exists between higher-level goals, development paths and daily/weekly activities.

Coaching—Coaching is a very important item in efforts to improve an employee's performance. Continuous performance offers a tool for managers to guide and drive coaching to others.

In addition, continuous performance is based on elements such as:

- ▶ 1:1 meeting that is the basis of continuous performance from a process perspective. It allows you to view all activities, topics, and coaching advice

- ▶ Notifications, which can include email, mobile and items on the to do list (tile)

- ▶ Notification if you have not updated your 1:1 meeting within a pre-defined period (employee)

- ▶ Notification if you have not met with the employee within a pre-defined period (manager)

- ▶ Annual summary where the most outstanding activities or items can be highlighted

Continuous performance is a tool that fundamentally changes the way performance is measured and tracked by allowing managers and employees to have constant feedback.

Employees can offer visibility to managers on activities and achievements in a very structured and measured way, while managers can provide feedback and offer constant support on all the different items the employee might be involved continually.

All of these, connected with the rest of the SuccessFactors suite can produce even more robust reports, feed more data into goals and development that will measure final performance, and used to make decisions about compensation and succession, and so on.

5.1.4   Cross-module integration

Other benefits with the performance module are the different cross-module opportunities.

SuccessFactors performance management can connect to:

- ▶ Compensation
- ▶ Employee profile
- ▶ Calibration
- ▶ Reporting

We will not cover details about them in this chapter, but these integration points will be discussed in other chapters about those topics.

To summarize, this module is very powerful and extensive. It offers organizations a very robust and flexible tool to handle performance reviews and more.

We learned how performance forms look in the system, analyzed each section, and learned a bit more about extra functionality like pods, writing assistant and integration opportunities.

Although we are dedicating a whole chapter to reporting, it is important to understand that basically everything in performance can be reported. It is critical to be able to report and understand all performance data to make better decisions.

Now let's learn more about calibration, which can be considered an addition to performance. Both modules work together.

6 Calibration

We continue diving deeper into the different talent management modules. Calibration is very special because can only work by grabbing data from other modules in a very similar way to employee profile.

Calibration is a process that generally takes place toward the end of a performance cycle. Its purpose is to standardize some of the performance level across the organization.

All this to avoid situations like the following:

▶ Managers having different expectations from their direct reports, so the highest performer in one team might be compared at the same level to the lowest performer in another team from a rating perspective with everything else equal.

▶ If an organization has a rating scale from 1–5 (as an example), and managers giving ratings skewed to one side or another by giving too many 1s, or too many 5s.

With calibration organizations have a tool to adjust ratings of individuals to ensure that performance levels are standardized across the enterprise.

Managers can see on a single screen different subjects of the calibration session (individuals from different teams), discuss between them—guided by a facilitator—and make decisions to standardize performance levels of employees.

Although in this book I am focusing on the calibration of performance, it can also be used for compensation and combined with succession too.

Let's learn how calibration works.

6.1 Overview

Calibration is also based on templates. In this case, they define what users will be seeing to perform the process of calibration.

Before digging deeper, let's clearly define the users of calibration. As mentioned, calibration is a tool for managers to meet and talk about their direct reports in order to standardize performance, compensation or succession data.

Imagine you are sitting in a room with your peers and you are talking about the overall performance of all direct reports of the group, ensuring that your best team member doesn't have the same score as the worst of someone else's rating (everything else equal).

Therefore, there are really two types of users for calibration sessions.

▶ Participants who are managers that will be discussing other people below the hierarchy.

▶ Facilitators who are most likely HR business partners that put the session together and coordinate the process.

Regular employees are part of the calibration process

 Technically regular employees, who are called subjects here, are part of the calibration process, but they are not users of the module.

In order to make this more real, let's imagine we are an HR business partner. I would go into calibration by clicking on the link from the home menu, as shown in Figure 6.1.

Then the HR business partner, or anyone conducting the session, will see all the calibration sessions they have been assigned to coordinate (Figure 6.2).

A calibration session is almost like a meeting, in which people attend. The purpose of the meeting is to discuss or calibrate either compensation, succession or performance data for people below the hierarchy of the session's participants.

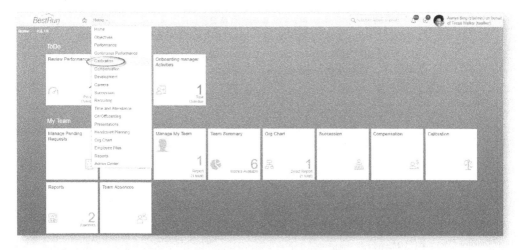

Figure 6.1: HR business partner accessing the calibration session

In Figure 6.2, we can see that I have three calibration sessions to be conducted.

Figure 6.2: Calibration home screen displaying calibration sessions

We can see very useful information such as:

▶ **Session's name**: Every time someone creates a session, it has to have a name. A good example can be "2017 Calibration session for IT analysts in the Southeast"

▶ **Template name**: This is the template used to create the actual session. This is relevant because each template might have different views and data.

For example, following the example earlier, we would like to calibrate IT analysts in the Southeast, but only performance and succession data (excluding compensation), we would know which template to use based on each name.

So, we could potentially have sessions that are called the same, but different templates.
a) 2017 Calibration session for IT analysts in the Southeast-performance template
b) 2017 Calibration session for IT analysts in the Southeast-compensation template

▶ **Status**: Each session will have a status based on the overall progress of the session. It can be approved, in progress, etc.

▶ **# Subjects**: Subjects are all employees that the calibration discussion will be based on. In other words, the people below the hierarchy of the session participants.

▶ **# of Participants**: Participants are people who will be performing the discussion and making calibration decisions for subjects.

▶ **Facilitators**: Facilitators are HR individuals who conduct the session as coordinators.

▶ **My role (s)**: This describes the role of the person looking at this screen.

▶ **Session date**: When the session has been scheduled.

▶ **Attachment**: Calibration allows adding relevant attachments to the session for everyone to view. This functionality is not often used, since truly everything you need to perform a good calibration session will be offered to you by the system.

Now that we understand the basics of calibration, let's see an actual session.

6.2 Calibration session

Once a user first enters a calibration session, they will be prompted by one dashboard view. Before we continue, it is important to define calibration views.

Views are not necessarily graphs, but very interactive user interfaces that display relevant data, and in some cases allow users to enter and change information about subjects.

6.2.1 Dashboard view

In Figure 6.3 we can see that this view is composed by two squares with numbers. These are 9-box matrix grids, just like those presented in the succession management chapter of this book.

Figure 6.3: Dashboard view in calibration

These two matrix grid reports show performance vs potential, and impact vs risk information.

Performance vs Potential is based on overall (performance) form rating vs overall potential (succession) rating as shown more closely on Figure 6.4.

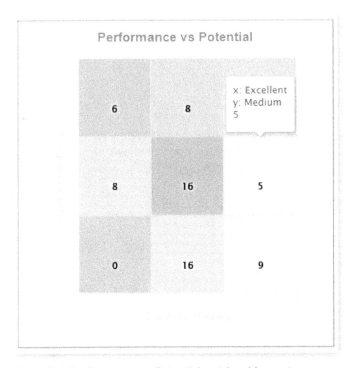

Figure 6.4: Performance vs Potential matrix grid report

If the user hovers over each box, it tells the user the X and Y axis.

In the very same fashion as the report above, impact vs risk is a matrix grid report that only works with succession data. It measures the risk of loss vs the impact of loss (Figure 6.5).

Colors and text can all be configured to match any culture, but the point of these two reports is that users will be able to see right away where the population of employees generally fall. This shapes a picture right away about the distribution of the different teams.

Let's see what other views are available.

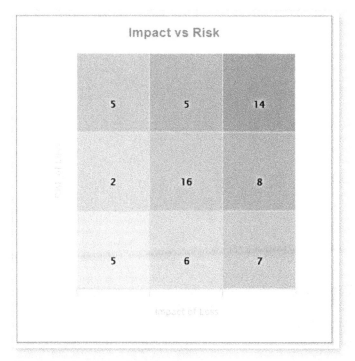

Figure 6.5: Impact vs risk report

6.2.2   List view

The list view is probably one of the most important.

Here a list of all subjects to be reviewed is presented to the participants. This information pretty much has everything needed for participants to set the stage for each discussion.

Figure 6.6 shows us how this list looks.

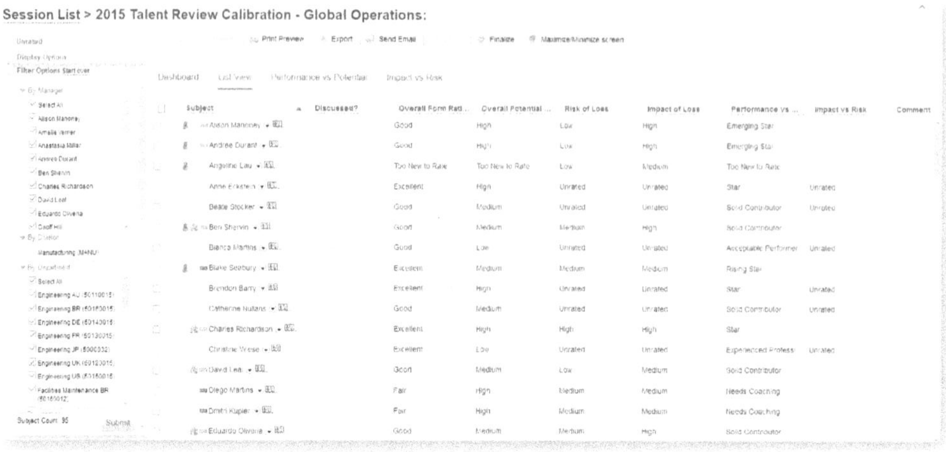

Figure 6.6: List view in calibration

On the left side, we can see the name of each subject to be reviewed/discussed. Then, moving right, we can see how information about performance and succession is presented.

So the calibration process will proceed like this. Let's say we are managers and we are calibrating for all IT analysts for the Southeast region. We would be either all (managers) sitting in a conference room looking at this screen and/or sharing screens via a conference call.

We begin with each subject, looking at the information presented. In case there needs to be able to see even more details about a particular employee, like in every other module, the employee quick card is available as shown in Figure 6.7, in which we can navigate directly to more information about the employee.

Obviously the purpose of calibration is to push toward a standard normal (bell-shaped) distribution, so here is probably the most important concept in calibration.

If and when we are ready to change a subject's information, we can just click on the value (rating) and simply change it. When this is changed in calibration, it will also push the change to the module from which the information came.

Figure 6.7: Employee quick card in calibration

For example, let's say we have decided to change Andree Durant's Overall Form Rating from "Good" (this is a value on the performance's rating scale) to "Excellent", and Risk of Loss from "Low" to "Medium".

As shown on Figure 6.8, we would simple click on the current ratings and select the new values.

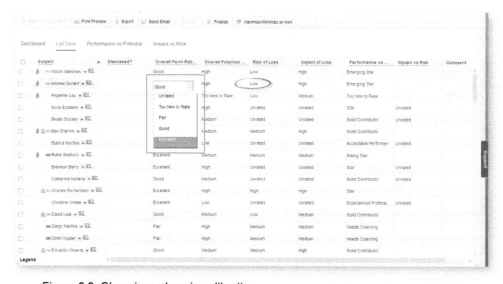

Figure 6.8: Changing values in calibration

125

In this case, once we make these changes, the performance form rating that originally had a rating for Andree of "Good" now would change to "Excellent", and same for succession data. Risk of loss would go from "Low" to "Medium".

After we have finished talking about a subject, we would mark the person as "discussed". A little green check mark will display right next to her name (Figure 6.9), to let participants know that the person has already been discussed and calibrated.

Figure 6.9: Discussion mark in calibration

Let's review other views available.

6.2.3   Performance vs potential

Do you remember earlier how the dashboard view had a Performance vs Potential and Impact vs Risk 9-box grid reports?

Well this view is the exact same report, however, with much more available. Let's look at Figure 6.10 to continue learning more about this view.

First of all you notice that the report looks much bigger, and contains information of who actually falls into each "bucket".

With this report, let's say we decide that there are too many subjects with high potential and excellent review, because that doesn't necessarily reflects the overall distribution of the organization.

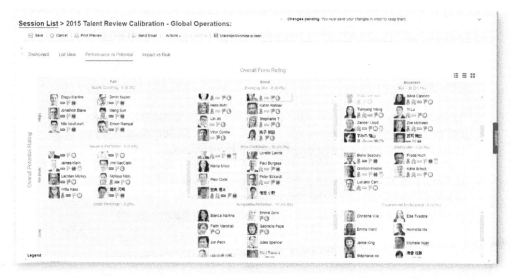

Figure 6.10: Performance vs Potential view in calibration

We can simply drag from one bucket and drop on another as shown in Figure 6.11 in which I am dragging Yi Lu from the "Star" bucket into "Emerging Star".

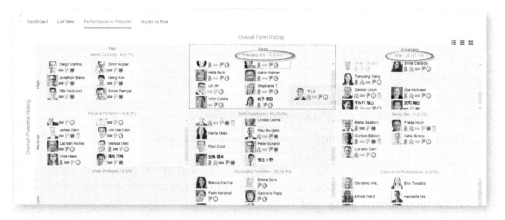

Figure 6.11: Dragging a subject from one bucket to another

Not only that, but just like with the previous view, by changing someone from one bucket to the other, the information that placed them there in the first place would automatically change too, in the modules from which the information came.

This become extremely handy in situations in which the process of calibration has happened or is happening, but then administrators have to go and manually adjust everyone's ratings. Here, everything is consolidated in one screen, so imagine how quickly and pain-free this process can become.

By this point you might be asking what the funny icons next to each subject are. Well, just like in the succession, each icon represents some type of information, category or criteria about the subject.

In Figure 6.12 we can see the company's legend (for the relationship between this icons and the information). This way it is much easier for someone to understand exactly other aspects of each subject.

Figure 6.12: Legend in 9-box matrix grid reports in calibration

As you can already imagine, this is a lot of information presented on a single screen, so participants can do a better assessment and calibrate in the most efficient way.

It gets even better. If someone clicks on a subject's picture (Figure 6.13), we can perform even more actions.

Figure 6.13: Additional actions on calibration

These actions allow participants to perform and/or review other information and activities about the subject, including:

- ▶ Provide a comment
- ▶ Open talent card (Figure 6.13)
- ▶ Edit talent review
- ▶ Employee profile
- ▶ Development
- ▶ Achievements (in continuous performance & goals)

Now that we have a solid foundation of the performance vs potential view, let's learn more about the impact vs risk view.

6.2.4 Impact vs risk

This view is almost exactly the same as the view reviewed earlier (performance vs potential), but it measures different information. In this case we are measuring all succession data (risk of loss vs impact of loss).

Figure 6.14 shows how this view looks.

Figure 6.14: Risk of loss vs impact of loss in calibration view

We will not repeat the functionality available, since it is exactly the same as the previous view; however, I will take the opportunity to explain some of the flexibility these views offer.

Let's start with the design of these matrix grid reports. The colors you see in the back of each bucket are configurable.

In addition, you can choose to utilize the icons next to each subject or not. Of course, you can define which icons you would like to utilize for each criteria and you can choose to only utilize a few (as opposed to utilizing all the ones available).

The name of each bucket can also be defined, and if we do not desire to display images of the subjects, we can change that too as shown in Figure 6.15.

What about displaying only subject's pictures (Figure 6.16).

Figure 6.15: Matrix grid report without subject pictures

Figure 6.16: Matrix grid report with only subject pictures

In summary, calibration is a very important module to support the overall talent management processes for existing employees.

I can guarantee 99% of organizations out there perform calibration processes; in many cases it might not be something formal, but I assure you it is there.

Well, with this powerful module, which brings together relevant information from potentially three different modules, there can be a formal calibration process that can be performed very quickly, intuitively and as efficiently as it gets, with a very powerful tool.

Although the information above was a very solid introduction, calibration can get even more robust and efficient by having distribution standards, custom views, etc. which are outside the scope of this introduction to SuccessFactors series; however, details are really meaningless unless we understand the basics. So as seen earlier, this module can generate quite a bit of value to any organization, even in its most simple usage.

With calibration under our belt, let's learn more about the big and important area of compensation management.

7 Compensation Management

Compensation management is one of my favorites (and the first module I ever implemented). This is all about compensation planning for the workforce.

I don't take for granted that everyone understands compensation planning, so I will briefly explain it.

Compensation planning is the process or action that reviews someone's current salary, in addition to other monetary rewards such as bonus and stock, and increases after a period of time (normally a year), or in some cases decreases too.

Normally the person in organizations who makes this decision is the direct manager, there are some that have different planning structures.

For the purpose of this book, we will work under the assumption that each manager plans total rewards for their direct reports since is the most common way.

Imagine you are a manager and have a team of five direct reports. It is the end of the year and time to perform compensation planning. At this point in the process the performance cycle has already happened. How do you go from here?

For some context, think about how this process is done for you currently. Do you use a system designed for this or just MS Excel? How is the information communicated? Is it effective?

All these questions are very important, because compensation planning is such an important process in an organization, but people only get one a year usually.

7.1 Compensation process

Let's start reviewing the actual compensation planning process.

In SuccessFactors an administrator would launch compensation work-sheets, which we will discuss in greater detail later in this chapter, to all compensation planners.

These planners depend on the compensation planner structure of the company, or can be selected one by one, etc., since the system is very flexible about this.

These planers would receive an email notification telling them that the time to plan for compensation has come. They would log into Success-Factors and select compensation from the home menu (Figure 7.1).

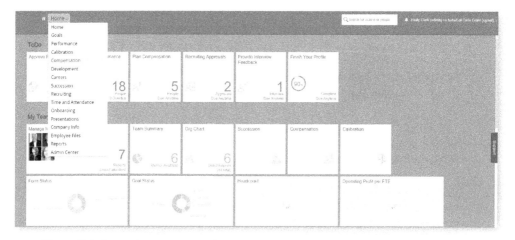

Figure 7.1: Accessing compensation

Then compensation planners will see all the plans they are responsible for, as shown in Figure 7.2.

For example, if someone is planning for salaried employees, that might be one compensation plan.

This planner could also be planning for salary increases for hourly peo-ple, this could be another plan, etc.

Once the planner clicks on the plan, they are taken to the actual work-sheet where the planning is performed.

Just like in performance management, there are always route maps as-sociated with compensation worksheets for approval/reviews.

Figure 7.2: Current compensation plans

Once the worksheets are completed and routed through the different stakeholders in the process, compensation statements can be generated for each employee finalizing the compensation planning process.

7.2 Compensation worksheet

As mentioned, a planner might be responsible for more than one compensation plan. Once the user clicks on each plan, the actual compensation worksheet for the plan opens up where the compensation planning happens.

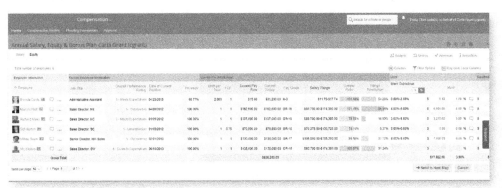

Figure 7.3: Compensation worksheet example

In Figure 7.3, we see what a compensation worksheet looks like.

Notice at the very beginning of the worksheet will display the names of all the people we are planning for. Again, normally managers would plan for their direct reports, but there are organizations that have different compensation planning structures.

The point is that in the worksheet all people who are eligible for compensation planning will be included.

Before we move on, let's talk about eligibility rules.

7.2.1 Eligibility rules

When we refer to eligibility rules, we are talking about all the potential rules that can be defined by administrators to determine who is eligible to receive compensation and who is not.

For example, let's say as an organization we have made the decision that anybody who was hired after October 31st is not eligible for compensation because they are too new. We would write a rule that grabs the employee's hire date (coming from employee profile) and tell the system to not include anyone with a hire date above 10/31/2017.

On another example, let's say we have managers who have direct reports all over the world, but because of the complexity of the compensation process for different locations, in this particular compensation plan we only want to include employees in the United States.

With the same idea, we would write a rule based on each employee's work location country and tell the system to only include the ones in the US.

Eligibility rules can be very flexible, handy and powerful. If you have ever been involved as an administrator for compensation in any organization, you know exactly what I am talking about.

To continue learning about the compensation worksheet, we go back to Figure 7.3 and can see that the next field over is job title. The point about this field is that in the compensation worksheet we can include any field we want, regardless if the data exists in SuccessFactors or not.

For example, let's say outside the data we currently have in employee profile, we would also like to present to compensation planners data we only have in our HRIS system such as current salary, we can have a daily import of data from the HRIS system into the compensation module (assuming Employee Central has not been implemented).

Therefore, any information the organization believes is important to present to compensation planners so they can make better compensation decision, can be displayed in the compensation worksheet.

It is important to mention that the order of the columns can change. As administrators, you have full control over these aspects of columns:

▶ Order

▶ Grouping

▶ Selection

▶ Data format

▶ Labels

The next field is the overall performance rating column (Figure 7.4).

Figure 7.4: Performance column in compensation worksheet

This is a very important column (field) because of the direct integration with performance management.

Before an administrator launches compensation forms to planners, we would define which performance template should be associated with which compensation plan. Normally you would have the ones for same year, so you would associate the "2017 Compensation Planning" template to the "2017 Performance Appraisal" form.

Compensation planning

 Compensation planning does not have to be integrated with performance.

The overall scores of the form would automatically display on the compensation worksheet, but not only that. If a planner clicks on the score, a pop-up window opens that shows the performance form for that particular employee (Figure 7.4).

7.2.2 Compensation guidelines

If your organization supports the concept of pay-for-performance, then whatever potential compensation award you receive will be based on your performance review.

This is where compensation guidelines are triggered. SuccessFactors compensation supports guidelines for any compensation award type, whether it is salary increase, lump sum, etc.

These guidelines can be very complex, built by very large matrixes. An example of a potential guideline could be:

Anybody with a job grade of IT10 working in the United States having a range penetration of 50% in the division of Information Technology with a rating of 3—Meets Expectations can have a salary increase between 1% and 3%.

You can imagine all the different combinations something like this could create. The good news is that SuccessFactors compensation supports all this. I have had clients with literally thousands of different guidelines.

As we continue with some of these fields, let's look closely at:

▶ Salary range

▶ Compa-Ratio

▶ Range penetration

Total number of employees: 6									
Employee Information		Current Pay Information							
↑ Employee		Units per Year	FTE	Current Pay Rate	Current Salary	Pay Grade	Salary Range	Compa-Ratio	Range Penetration
Brenda Davis		2,080	1	$15.00	$31,200.00	H-3	$11.75-$17.74	101.69%	54.26%
Marcus Hoff		1	1	$162,500.00	$162,500.00	GR-16	$93,700.00-$174,300.00	121.18%	85.36%
Richard Maxx		1	1	$107,000.00	$107,000.00	GR-16	$93,700.00-$174,300.00	79.79%	16.50%
Sid Morton		1	0.75	$70,500.00	$70,500.00	GR-16	$70,275.00-$130,725.00	70.10%	0.37%
Wilma Sown		1	1	$130,000.00	$130,000.00	GR-17	$105,000.00-$195,200.00	86.55%	27.72%
Vic Stokes		1	1	$135,000.00	$135,000.00	GR-16	$93,700.00-$174,300.00	100.67%	51.24%
	Group Total				$636,200.00				

Items per page 50 ⌄   Page 1   of 1

Figure 7.5: Additional fields

In addition to all potential fields that we could have in our worksheet, Salary range, Compa-Ratio, Range penetration, are fields that add extra value to any plan.

These columns (compa-ratio and range penetration) show a nice colored bar for a more user-friendly display.

Up to this point we have only focused on fields that are considered in-formation-only fields.

Let's take a step back and understand this better. If you are a compensa-tion planner, and you are responsible for determining how much money your team will get in salary increases, lump sums, etc., you probably would like to have as much relevant information as possible to be able to make a more rational decision.

Let's take a look at some of the other fields that make up this particular worksheet.

SuccessFactors compensation is not limited

By no mean SuccessFactors compensation is limited to the fields discussed in this chapter. There are dozens of standard fields available in addition to the hundreds of potential custom fields a company might need to support their compensation planning efforts.

In Figure 7.6 we can start seeing some fields that are open for input data. These are all very self-explanatory.

Figure 7.6: Compensation planning fields

There are over one hundred screenshots in this book, however, Figure 7.6 is one screenshot you should review in detail.

If you have ever done compensation planning, I invite you to admire Figure 7.6. If you have done it in Excel, just think how much easier, quicker, more efficient, and user-friendly the SuccessFactors compensation worksheet is.

We can enter merit increase percentages, based on guidelines that can be hard or soft. Any adjustments can be entered and their impact seen at the bottom, and much more.

SuccessFactors compensation, along with performance management, are probably the most mature modules of the entire talent suite. I could literally talk all day about compensation and show you every little feature

140

and functionality available in the module, but that would probably take a whole dedicated book.

Now that we understand how a compensation planning worksheets look, let's stay in the worksheet, but let's discuss other features available here for compensation planners.

7.2.3   Compensation worksheet—additional features

Outside all the information fields (columns) in the compensation worksheet that empower planners with the right information to make good compensation planning decisions, there are some additional features within the worksheet that are equally important.

Let's begin talking about budgets.

Compensation budgets

Of course it would be very nice to be able to award our team with unlimited salary increases to reward them for their hard work and keep them motivated, but there are limits. In compensation these are called budgets and of course, SuccessFactors compensation supports them.

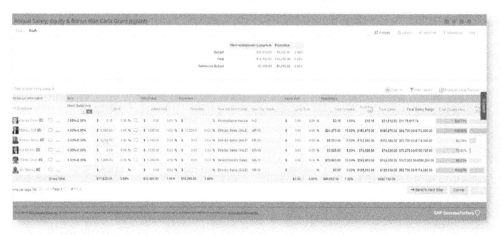

Figure 7.7: Compensation worksheet budget

If we look at Figure 7.7, we can see that on top it displays a budget I set up for this compensation plan.

Budgets are very flexible. We can set a single budget at top and cascade it down the organization. We can also base these budgets on a hard amount, percentages of a value (based salaries for the team, etc.) or many other criteria.

Budgets can also be set to be hard or soft. If a budget is hard, the system will not let you move to the next step in the route map unless your compensation recommendation are within budgets. With soft budgets, it might give you a warning if you are above budget, but would still let you move on.

	Merit+Adjustment+LumpSum	Promotion	
Budget	$31,810.00	$9,400.00	2.00%
Total	$30,312.00	$16,250.00	3.46%
Remaining Budget	$1,498.00	-$6,850.00	-1.46%

Figure 7.8: Budget example

Budgets are very simple as shown in Figure 7.8. If you think about it, compensation planners already have so much information in one screen, and then have to worry about budget calculations; that can put a true toll into the whole process and user experience, so SuccessFactors makes it easier.

Budgets get calculated in real-time once you are making your recommendations so the planner knows exactly where he/she is getting.

Budgets can also be a combination of compensation elements. In case of Figure 7.8, I had combined the amount awarded for merit, adjustment and lump sum to be a single budget, and the promotion fields a separate budget.

Let's take a look at metrics now.

Compensation metrics

Pay-for-performance is now pretty much the standard in competitive organizations.

SuccessFactors definitely embraces that concept, and the compensation worksheet offers some nice charts that tell the planner where the team resides with the current recommendations.

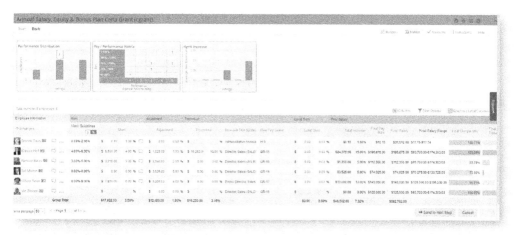

Figure 7.9: Pay-for-performance metrics

With Figure 7.9, we see there are three graphs available that summarizes performance ratings of subjects being planned and the relationship with current compensation recommendations with these insights about people being planned.

- ▶ Performance distribution
- ▶ Pay-for-performance relationship (matrix of compa-ratio vs overall performance)
- ▶ Actual merit increase given.

Let's now review the workflow, or route map of this particular compensation plan.

Route map

Just like in performance management, compensation plans always have a route map (or workflow of approval) associated with them.

Figure 7.10: Compensation plan route map

We see a case in Figure 7.10 where the worksheet is currently on the first step. As a planner, once I am finished with my compensation recommendations, dictated by this route map, the form would be moved to an approval step. Then it moves to a step in which the compensation administrator reviews it, and then the form is completed.

Flexible route maps

Route maps are extremely flexible. Administrators can have as many steps as they want and pretty much configure everything within the route map.

Different compensation plans might have different route maps associated with them. For example, in the United States, it is required that the VP of Compensation review all recommendations. However in Latin America, because they are so restricted with guidelines, there is no review from senior leadership. Therefore we would probably have two compensation plans, one for United States with one route map, and another for Latin America with another route map.

Now that we have an understanding of route maps within compensation worksheets, let's review the compensation profile.

Compensation profile

As you probably noticed so far, SuccessFactors compensation offers all the relevant information and right tools for planners to perform a compensation recommendation, all in a single screen; however, it we think about it, a planner might have all the people being planned for in a single screen, but at the moment of planning, they are performing the action individual by individual.

Because of this fact, the compensation profile exists within the worksheet. If we remember from the figures above, the first column of the compensation worksheet is the subject's name.

If a user clicks on the name, a window pops up with the compensation profile as shown in Figure 7.11.

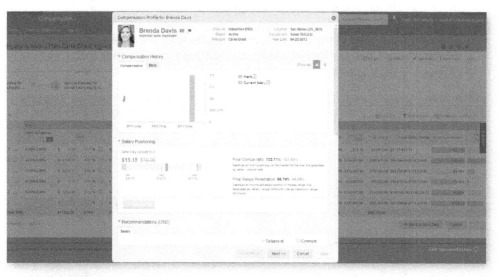

Figure 7.11: Compensation profile

The Compensation profile is a very dynamic and interactive way of performing compensation recommendations.

On the very top, we can see the employee's picture and some basic recommendation. Then right underneath, the planner can see historical compensation data for the employee. This data comes from past compensation templates (most likely from past years). This historical data can display in a bar chart or as line items.

Then, the planner can see information about compa-ratio and range penetration in addition to an explanation of what those compensation concepts mean:

Compa-ratio: Describes an individual's pay vs the median for the role. It is calculated as salary / median rate.

Range penetration: Describes an individual's salary position in the pay range. It is calculated as (salary—range minimum) / (range maximum—range minimum).

If the planner continues scrolling down, the exact same information presented in the compensation worksheet would be displayed, including the recommendation fields as shown in Figure 7.12.

The whole purpose of the compensation profile is to offer the exact same information as the worksheet would do, but have the planner focus exclusively on a single individual at a time.

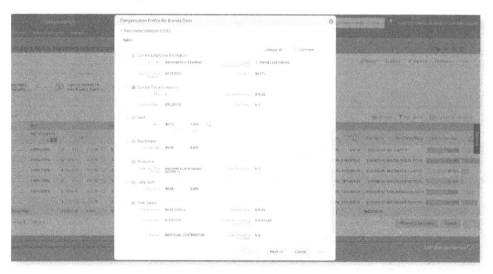

Figure 7.12: Recommendation fields in compensation profile

Of course every time a planner makes a change in the compensation profile, the change automatically gets reflected in the compensation worksheet.

With the compensation profile under our belt, let's review some of the other functionality available in the system.

Additional Features

In addition to the features discussed earlier, the compensation worksheet allows planners to:

▶ Print compensation worksheet

▶ Filter subjects based on several criteria as shown in Figure 7.13.

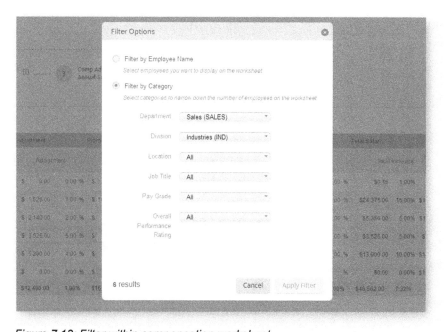

Figure 7.13: Filter within compensation worksheet

▶ Hide certain columns from the view

Another very important point is the fact that SuccessFactors compensation supports multiple currencies. Not only that, but this concept is dy-

147

namic. Let's say a manager resides in the United States, but he is planning for individuals in Latin America, Europe and the Middle East.

SuccessFactors compensation accommodates this in a very efficient way. Looking at Figure 7.14 we see that the system allows planners to toggle between currency views.

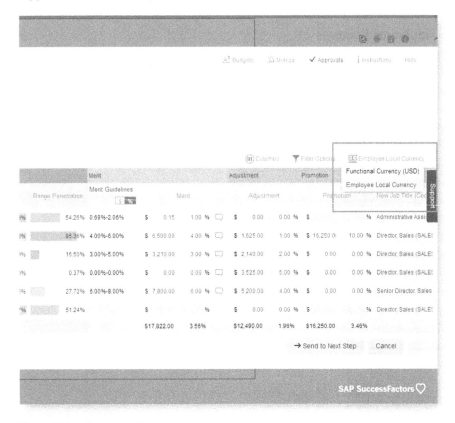

Figure 7.14: Currency views

In the system there will always be a functional currency setup, which is normally the currency in which the company reports on, but SuccessFactors understands that teams are global and therefore it standardizes the currency challenges. It offers the opportunity for planners to plan in:

▶ Functional currency—all US dollars, assuming the company's functional currency is United States.

▶ Employee local currency—it will convert values to employee's local currency, while maintaining the functional currency. So for instance, if I am a manager who resides in the United States, but I have a direct report who I am planning for in India, and I award her a 12% salary increase (I know right!), I can toggle to employee's local currency and see exactly how much Indian rupees that 12% is (and vice versa).

▶ Manager's local currency—although not shown in the screenshots, lets planners plan everything in their local currency (which is what they know best), and the system performs the calculations in the backend.
Therefore, if I am a planner located in the Netherlands and I am planning for my team who resides in Chile, United States and India, I would plan in Euros and then toggle to see how much my recommendation means in the different currencies.

With currencies, we pretty much covered everything basic about the compensation worksheet.

So, let's pretend we have finished the compensation planning process, and it has gone through the necessary approval. What's next?

Let's talk about how to communicate compensation planning results with employees by learning about compensation statements next.

7.3   Compensation statements

As mentioned earlier, we understand that compensation is all about performing planning compensation elements such as salary increases, lump sum, bonuses, etc. for employees down the hierarchy. One important point that we cannot miss is how the entire process is finalized.

If we think about it, let's say someone in your team got a salary increase of 5% effective January 1st.; obviously this information would have to be sent somehow to the HRIS system, so it can be processed by payroll; however, that's a topic for another day.

For now we will focus on how to communicate to employees, in this case, communicate to a direct report that she got an increase of 5%. The solution SuccessFactors compensation offers is the compensation statement.

Figure 7.15: Compensation statement example.

Figure 7.15 shows how this compensation statement is almost like we had created it in MS Word or PDF as it is normally done, but in this case if was automatically generated.

We see how the statement will always have your company logo at the very top, in addition to a title. Obviously we would want to have a compensation statement for every compensation cycle.

Then, after the title, there will be an opportunity to enter text, which most likely will be a note from leadership to employees with a signature at the bottom.

In addition, toward the right of the statement, all the relevant compensation information will be displayed, which is equivalent to fields in the worksheet. For instance, let's say in our worksheet we have configured a column that says Last Year's Increase, that column could also display here.

Essentially any data in any column in the compensation worksheet can display as a field in this portion of the compensation statement.

Also there can by rules written to elements in compensation statements; for example, we only want to show the field Total Raise to employees who actually got a raise, and not display it for employees who did not get any raise. We could easily do this by writing rules and conditions in the compensation statement.

Now remember that these compensation statements are automatically generated to the entire user population who was part of this particular compensation cycle. So if we have 120,000 employees who the organization performed compensation planning for globally, all of them would get a compensation statement, matching their particular data, with the click of a single button.

Compensation statement administration

When I say that they get automatically generated, we meant that this happens once an administrator actually generates statements. Also, there is a huge level of security regarding who can see these statements.

It is important to mention too, that compensation statements can be recalled in case there are any issues.

Do you remember back in the employee profile chapter, how we defined employee profile as almost your employee folder with all your employee data; well, compensation statements are not the exception.

Once compensation statements are generated, they will be available in employee profile based on permissions as shown in Figure 7.16.

Compensation statement employee visibility

Normally companies would want to have employees see their own statements.

Also, managers see their direct report's statements. HR business part-ners might want to see their population statements. All these authoriza-tions (and more) can be configured.

Figure 7.16: Compensation statements in employee profile

In Figure 7.16 we see a section in employee profile dedicated to compensation statements, and also how compensation statements from past cycles stack over each other.

If a user clicks on each statement a new browser tab opens with the actual statement. This statement can also be printed or saved as a PDF file.

Before closing this chapter, I want to mention that the compensation worksheet is very flexible regarding information to display, input, logic, and calculations; therefore, it is common to use compensation to also plan for bonus and stock awards, even though the variable pay module is designed to accommodate for this.

SuccessFactors compensation is one of the most mature and robust modules of the entire suite. It allows companies to standardize and utilize a system that simplifies a process that can be extremely complicated such as compensation planning.

With the basics of compensation management under our belt, let's learn more about variable pay.

8 Variable pay

I must confess that this became a separate chapter towards the end of writing this book. The reason is because variable pay might be considered an add-on to the compensation management module in my opinion.

Essentially its core functionality is the same as compensation management with differences really regarding processes and types of compensation elements.

Compensation management focuses more on salary increases, lump sums, adjustments, etc. versus variable pay; just like the name says, it's about those compensation awards that vary such as bonuses and stock awards.

At the end of the day variable pay does have unique functionality, or extra functionality compared to compensation, which is the main reason I decided to make it a chapter.

This should be a shorter chapter since the base features (worksheets, compensation fields, compensation statements, etc.) were highlighted under compensation; in this chapter we will only focus on the extra features and functionality variable pay offers for bonuses and stock awards.

8.1   Overview

Variable pay includes any employee compensation that is not paid in equal proportions through the year compared to salary increases, in addition to being components that reward employees for their direct contributions toward company goals.

Just like compensation, the high-level variable pay process follows these steps:

1. Setup bonus plans and rules for bonus payout
2. Determine eligibility of employees and calculate pro-rated bonus payouts
3. Approve bonus payout and generate statements

Let's look into more details in a variable pay worksheet.

Like other modules, a user with the correct authorization would access variable pay worksheets by going into compensation from the home menu (Figure 8.1).

Figure 8.1: Access compensation and variable pay

Once in compensation, users will see a list of all the compensation and/or variable pay worksheets they are responsible for completing or approving as shown in Figure 8.2.

Figure 8.2: Compensation and variable pay worksheets

To be honest, there is not really a way to determine whether a worksheet is for compensation or variable pay on this screen; however, normally each plan would be called something relevant to the type of compensation to be planned.

For example, if it has the word "equity" or "bonus" in the name, most likely it is a variable pay worksheet.

8.1.1   Variable pay worksheet

Once the user clicks to begin variable pay planning, a worksheet will open just like in compensation, but this worksheet looks slightly different.

Figure 8.3: Variable pay worksheet

Let's start learning about each component.

On this particular worksheet we are allocating individual bonuses. At the center of the screen, toward the left, the name and image of all people being planned are displayed in a bar chart on Figure 8.4.

157

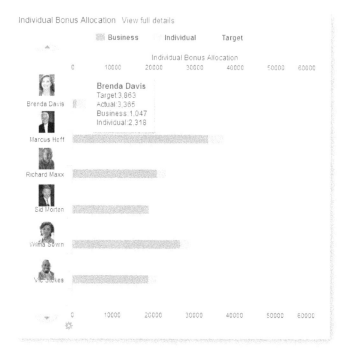

Figure 8.4: Variable pay worksheet bar chart.

This bar chart represents the numbers for the business, individual, and target. Notice that if someone hovers over a subject's bar, the actual numbers display.

Let's not focus too much on the numbers, because the criteria and actual numbers can change to match your organization. For example we can only compare target and individual (actual) if we want.

Obviously all targets and actual numbers are imported into the system by your compensation administrator (data coming most likely from your ERP and/or accounting system).

This graph can also be displayed as traditional columns as shown in Figure 8.5.

In addition, the numbers here, like compensation, support different currencies so the planner can toggle between currencies and actual currency conversion table performed in real-time for calculations behind the scenes.

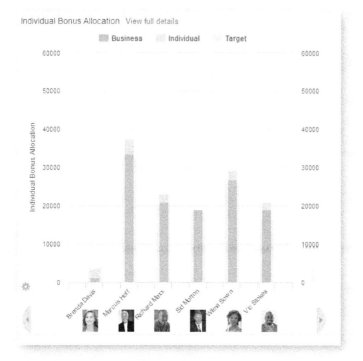

Figure 8.5: Column bar chart

Currency conversion tables

 The currency conversion table is controlled by administrators, which can be updated as many times as desired, but normally companies will update it every month or so.

The subjects in the graph can also be sorted by:

▶ Name

▶ Final payout

▶ Ascending

▶ Descending

If we refer back to Figure 8.3, we notice that toward the right side of the variable pay worksheet, there are blocks of other useful information.

Let's look at some of them.

8.1.2   Budget

The budget "portlet" is the first section to appear in this view of the variable pay worksheet (Figure 8.6).

Figure 8.6: Budget section in variable pay

The budget section displays graphically the budget amount for the component being planned. In this case we are planning for individual bonuses so in this case the system is telling the planner that they can allocate about $1.25 million dollars in bonuses for this particular team.

Again, the budget is fully controlled by the compensation administrator and can be very flexible to accommodate any potential budget scenario your company might need. I feel very comfortable saying that since I have implemented SuccessFactors compensation management for many companies ranging in size from large Fortune 25 enterprises to smaller businesses with 5000 employees, and I have never had issues accommodating budgets; regardless of how complex some of them might be.

In addition to the potential budget amount, the graph shows that the current allocated amount (represented by the "green" bar) is below our budget.

If we were allocating above budget, this would display in red on the graph, but it would depend on guidelines whether we can go above budget or not.

8.1.3 Exceptions

The next section on this variable pay view is the exceptions portlet (Figure 8.7).

Figure 8.7: Exception section in variable pay worksheet

The exception section lets the planner know if there is any "outlier" within the current plan, based on the people eligible for this plan.

In this case, the system is telling the planner that there are four individuals within this current plan that are "over target (bonus)". This exception is based on the amount that has been planned for these individuals here in the variable pay plan compared against the target amount, which just like compensation can be based on many different variables including:

▶ Performance scores

▶ Sales targets

▶ Company multiplier

▶ Division multiplier

▶ Any other special rule

In this case, the system is also letting the planner know that there is one individual whose current allocation is actually under target.

161

8.1.4   Employee details

The next section corresponds to employee details as shown in Figure 8.8.

Figure 8.8: Employee profile section in variable pay worksheet

This section allows the variable pay planner to look at employee's details coming directly from employee profile. This refers to the basic employee data.

In this case the user can see:

▶   The name of subject being planned

▶   Their title

▶   Ability to add comments

▶   Whether the person is eligible for promotion (rules written in the backend)

▶   Work tenure

▶   Impact of loss (coming from succession module)

▶   Current total & target payout

Under the employee profile section in the worksheet, additionally at the bottom we can find business-related data.

Figure 8.9: Business section in variable pay worksheet

As already mentioned we can see information about total and target payout, but also supporting information like:

▶ Dates of the plan

▶ Business information

  ▶ Earnings before taxes, interest, depreciation and amortization (EBITDA)

  ▶ Business unit (BU) revenue

  ▶ Business unit (BU) customer satisfaction

  ▶ Index

Notice that this data is how a particular system was configured. If someone wanted to display other metrics such as margins, profits, etc. it can absolutely be configured.

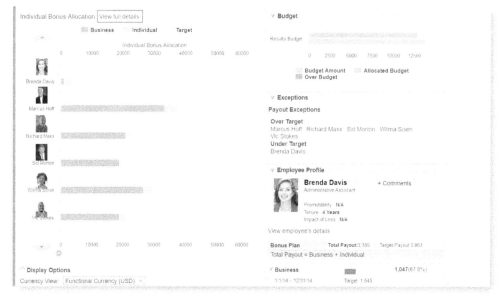

Figure 8.10: View full details in variable pay worksheet

We already mentioned that I consider variable pay an add-on to compensation. The reason for this was the fact that variable pay at its core is very similar to compensation.

Everything you have read in this chapter has been focused on the additional functionality variable pay offers compared to compensation, but we did mention where they were similar.

On top of the variable pay worksheet, there is a link "View Full Details" (Figure 8.10).

When clicked, you would be taken to a screen just like compensation, but only with variable pay data (the exact same data shown on the earlier image).

As shown in Figure 8.11, we can see that the variable pay worksheet turns into the same style as a compensation worksheet.

The main benefit of using this view is that all information displayed on the other view would display here, but also any custom field added to the variable pay worksheet would also display here.

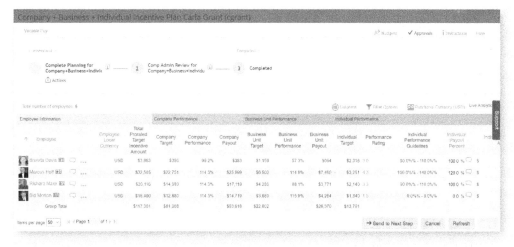

Figure 8.11: View more details on variable pay worksheet

If you noticed from the figures at the beginning of the chapter, pretty much everything displayed there was standard functionality.

Any custom fields, whether used for information purposes and/or for calculations would only be available on this screen.

Needless to say, variable pay benefits from all platform-related functionality (just like other modules), includes permissions, reporting, cross-module integration, etc.

With this, we finish our exploration of variable pay. To summarize, variable pay allows users to perform planning on variable compensation, mainly including stock/equity awards and bonuses.

This leverages quite a bit of functionality from compensation, but it also includes its own capability and functionality that offers all necessary tools for planners to perform variable pay actions the most efficiently and effectively as possible.

Let's go over one of the most interactive modules by learning about succession management next.

9 Succession management

Succession management is a very powerful module. It is designed to create and maintain succession plans across the organization, and provide features and functionality to support the "why" of nominations to persons or roles that make up a succession plan among many other things.

The key element of succession is the succession org chart, commonly called "SOC".

This org chart is quite similar to the regular hierarchy org chart discussed in Chapter 2, but instead of a hierarchical structure, this org chart also shows users successors or nominees.

In this chapter we will analyze the following tools available that make up succession management:

- ▶ Succession org chart
- ▶ Lineage chart
- ▶ Talent pools
- ▶ Talent search
- ▶ 9-box matrix grid reports

The actual visuals are very user-friendly and interactive, and it would take a whole book to explain them all in detail. The information that follows will be more than enough to have a solid understanding overall about what it can do.

Before going into details, I would like to mention cross-integration. This module literally leverages functionality that belongs to other modules for it to be functional. For example, the 9-box grid cannot be used without information from performance (and goals) management and employee profile.

I mention this because succession is the perfect module to continue showcasing how beautiful and powerful SuccessFactors can become once modules start to talk to each other.

Let's begin reviewing the succession org chart.

9.1 Succession org chart

The succession org chart is the backbone of succession, and the center-piece in which the succession plan for the organization is tracked.

Looking at Figure 9.1 we see that it looks like a regular org chart with the organization hierarchy structure, but users can clearly see who has been nominated as successor for a particular individual.

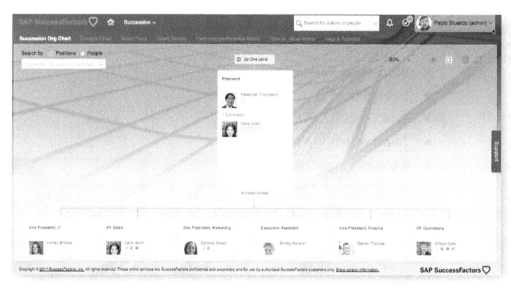

Figure 9.1: Succession org chart

Position-based succession nominations

 There are different types of nomination structures for the succession plan. These can be based on a person or position. In this book we will base all discussions on position-based nomination, which means a nominee should be ready to take a position rather than succeed someone.

For example if Marcus Hoff is nominated for the position of VP Sales, which is currently occupied by Carla Grant, Marcus is defined to succeed anyone in that position (whether Carla or someone else), rather than to succeed Carla specifically. If Carla moved to another position, Marcus would still remain as a successor for that position.

Essentially how the succession org chart works as the instrument to track the succession plan for the organization is by having a user (with proper permissions):

1. Go to the succession org chart

2. Find a position this user would like to nominate someone (I can find myself and define my potential successor).

3. Click on the position and search for either:
   a. Someone in the organization
   b. An external candidate

4. Add information about the nominee such as:
   a. Readiness
   b. Ranking
   c. Any development goals
   d. Notes

5. Review other information (from employee profile)

Figure 9.2 illustrates the actions above.

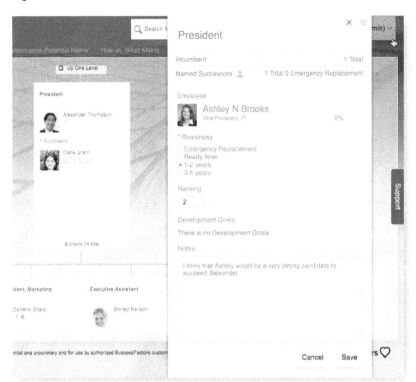

Figure 9.2: Nominating Ashley Brooks to President Position

Integration point between recruiting and succession

 Searching for an external candidate is an integration point with recruiting. Essentially we would be telling our recruiters that we are nominating someone who just applied to a job requisition, or someone who needs to apply or be added to the candidate pool. This plays very nicely with the employee referral functionality in recruiting management (part two).

If we look at Figure 9.3, we can see that now for the President position there are two nominees:

1. Carla Grant

2. Ashley Brooks (we just nominated her)

Figure 9.3: Nomination of Ashley Brooks

With this example, we can begin understanding how the succession plan begins to shape.

Let's imagine the following scenario. Alexander Thompson has just informed the board of directors that he is planning to step away as the President & CEO of the company in 2 years.

HR can come to SuccessFactors, see who has been defined as a successor to the position, and learn all kinds of information about the nominees, bringing data from employee profile (work experience, languages, and education), performance data, and more.

Now that we have a better understanding of the succession org chart and how it works, let's learn about the lineage chart.

9.2   Lineage chart

Lineage chart, just like its name, displays the actual succession plan of the organization. If we look at Figure 9.4, we can see the succession plan for three positions.

Figure 9.4: Lineage chart

To follow with the example provided earlier, in which we nominated as successor Ashley Brooks to the position of President, we can clearly see in Figure 9.4 that Ashley Brooks now is associated to Alexander Thompson (because he is the position holder).

Nomination vs. successors

 You will notice that in the "box" for the position, it lists "nominations" and "successor". Succession allows to set up an approval process in order to nominate individuals as successors. If we had a pending nomination (someone nominated a person, but who still needs to be approved), it would show up as a nomination.

Lineage chart is dynamic, meaning that a click on any position will then display the successors for that particular position as shown in Figure 9.5.

Figure 9.5: Marcus Hoff's lineage chart

We can see that now it displays Marcus Hoff's lineage chart.

You will notice that in addition to the search functionality on the left side of the screen, there is also a small icon next to each person's name; both in search results and lineage chart itself. This icon opens up the quick card (discussed in Chapter 2), which allows to see basic information about the employee and allows different actions as shown in Figure 9.6.

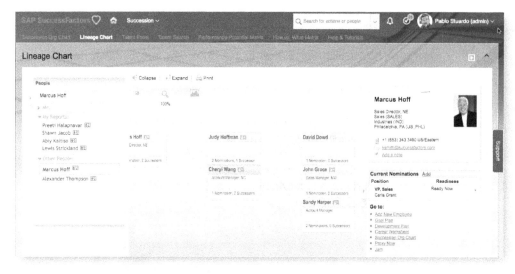

Figure 9.6: Quick card in lineage chart

Notice too that each person is colored based on their level of readiness to take the position.

Although a simple concept, the lineage chart can be very useful for looking at succession plans.

Let's discuss talent pools next.

9.3   Talent pools

Talent pools essentially allow key users to be grouped together that might fall under a certain criteria. If we look at Figure 9.7, we see that for this particular system there are two talent pools.

- ▶ **Sales talent pipeline**: groups people that can be promoted to higher sales roles.

- ▶ **Fall management rotation program**: groups people who will be part of the organization's management program.

There is no limit to the number of talent pools organizations can have; although they are designed to group people for succession-related reasons, they can be used however you want (like the fall management program reviewed earlier).

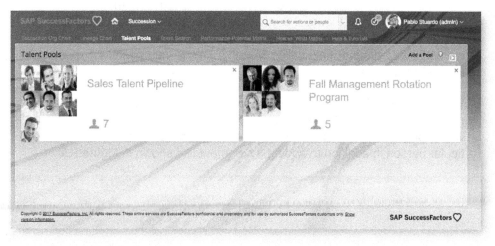

Figure 9.7: Talent pools

Once the user clicks (Figure 9.8) on the each talent pool, a new screen will be presented with all members of that particular talent pool and their level of readiness (again thinking from the standpoint of ready-to-succeed someone).

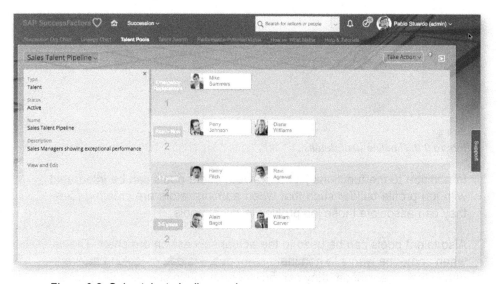

Figure 9.8: Sales talent pipeline pool

Once the talent pool is opened, on the left side you see the talent pool information. An important detail to keep in mind is that the data fields you see there (type, status, name, etc.) can be modified or admins can add or remove fields. In Figure 9.8 where we are tracking sales managers with exceptional performance, if we would also like to track their mobility, we could add another field called Mobility. This is very useful for reporting on talent pools.

Within Figure 9.8 we see how each subject is grouped based on readiness, but not only that. If we click on someone's image, a small window will display allowing a user to change the level of readiness of that particular person in addition to adding a comment like shown in Figure 9.9.

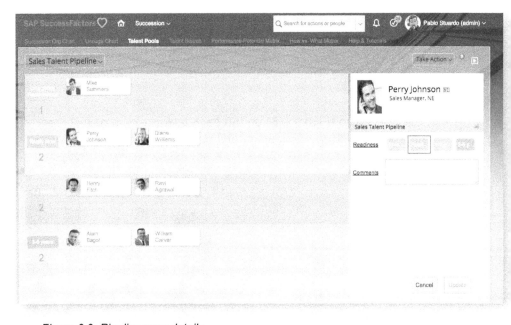

Figure 9.9: Pipeline user details

In addition to the functions just explained, talent pools can be integrated with job profile builder such that when administrators are creating roles, they can associate those job profiles to talent pools.

Also talent pools can be used in the actual succession org chart. That is, when someone wants to nominate someone, instead of looking at everyone in the organization, they can only search within specific talent pools.

Now that you have a good understanding of talent pools, let's learn more about probably my favorite tool in the entire SuccessFactors suite, talent search.

9.4 Talent search

Talent search can be used as a stand-alone tool, but it is grouped with succession. It empowers HR managers, department managers, leadership, or any user to search for talent (people) within the organization.

If we take a step back and think about it, nowadays companies are global and very complex; projects are expensive and risky, and some job roles are critical to the survival of the organization.

Therefore, it is absolutely critical for HR leaders to have a tool that allows them to conduct talent searches, then view and compare employees based on different criteria.

The need to staff complex projects, move people to different roles, and make global assignments requires a tool that can yield accurate search information, but at the same time needs to be a tool that is simple to use.

With talent search, users can search for any element of data that might exist in the system.

This includes the following categories:

9.4.1 Personal and organizational

▶ Division, department, location, etc.

▶ Mobility status

▶ Future leader, risk of loss, etc.

▶ Any field you might have for personal information in employee profile

Figure 9.10: Basic information in talent search

9.4.2 Background information

▶ Language skills

▶ Formal education

▶ Work experience

▶ Leadership experience

▶ Career goals

▶ Any background information you might have in employee profile

Figure 9.11: Background information in talent search

9.4.3 Trends

▶ Performance trend

▶ Potential trend

▶ Any competency

▶ Any trend data that might exist in the system

Trend data in SuccessFactors

When we talk about trend data in the system, we refer to any data that historically changes. For instance, performance is trend data because users will have a rating (potentially different) every performance cycle.

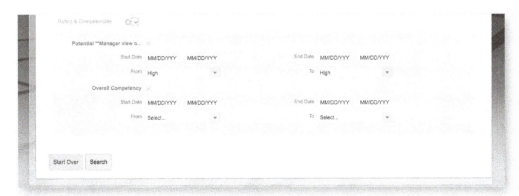

Figure 9.12: Trend data in talent search

After the users decided upon the search criteria to be used, the search results will appear as shown in Figure 9.13.

179

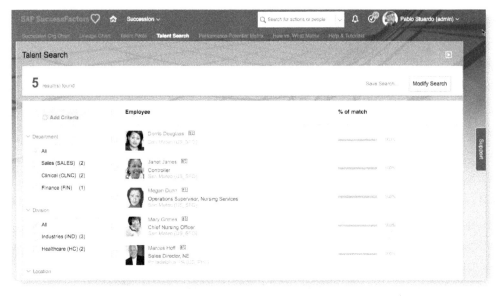

Figure 9.13: Talent search results screen

As you can see, a list of users matching the search criteria will display with its percentage of match.

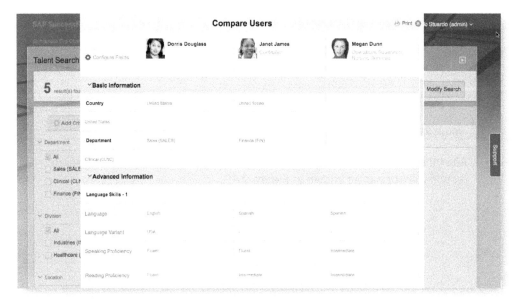

Figure 9.14: Search comparison talent search

In addition, you can compare many users at a time. The way it works, is by you selecting the users you would like to compare, and then all the information (used in the search criteria) will display like shown in Figure 9.14.

9.4.4 Other features

Talent search also offers the ability to nominate successors or add candidates to a talent pool directly from the search results (Figure 9.15).

Figure 9.15: Search results—other features

While nominating a successor, a new screen displays to define the position for which we are trying to nominate users; we can add their level of readiness as well as ranking and any notes as shown in Figure 9.16.

Figure 9.16: Nominate directly from talent search results

The last item worth mentioning about Talent Search is that results can also be exported in MS Excel format (Figure 9.17).

Figure 9.17: Export talent search results

As mentioned earlier, talent search is my personal favorite tool in the entire system, because of its robustness and how extremely useful it can be for many key resources in the organization.

Let's learn more about a rather fun functionality next.

9.5   9-Box matrix grid reports

The 9-box matrix grid reports place individuals based on two axes. Look at Figure 9.18 to understand the concept better.

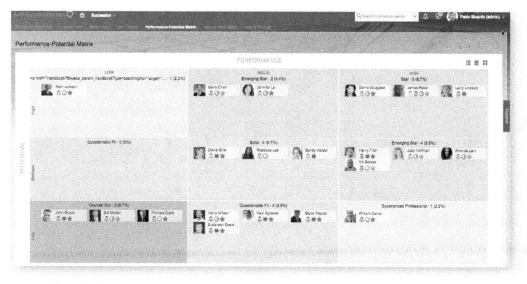

Figure 9.18: Performance-potential matrix grid

Matrix report size

 Actually this 9-box matrix grid (3×3), can technically be configured to be 4×4 or even 5×5. This is not recommended because it affects negatively the user interface and resolution of the matrix.

You might be asking yourself, where is the information coming from? Well, remember back in Chapter 2, we talked about employee profile and how it is like a folder with all documentation about employees?

For fields such as potential, this information is maintained in employee profile by each manager or leader. For instance, a normal business case is to have senior managers update the potential, risk of loss, etc. for their teams.

183

In Figure 9.19 we see how a manager, in this case Richard Maxx, would update succession in one of our blocks (in a view) in employee profile.

Figure 9.19: Update information in employee profile

As for performance, the data is coming from the final overall performance rating given in a particular cycle; it can be configured which template the system is looking at.

You also notice that next to each person there are a few icons. These icons are the graphical representation of some information about each employee. For example, in my system I have configured a green circle with a white "L" in the middle to represent a value of low for field risk of loss.

In Figure 9.20 I have opened the ledger in the matrix report.

In addition, if we click on each employee's photo, detailed information will show about the employee (all coming from employee profile) as shown in Figure 9.21.

Figure 9.20: Ledger icons on matrix grid report

Figure 9.21: Additional information in 9-box report

I would also like to mention that this is considered a report and can be printed like almost anything in the system. In Figure 9.21 we see how this would look. Also these reports can of course be downloaded in PDF format.

Figure 9.22: Print matrix grid reports

It is important to mention too that these reports have quite a bit of flexibility:

▶ The label on each box can be changed

▶ The overall report can be bigger (4x4 or 5x5—although not recommended)

▶ The colors for the boxes can be adjusted

▶ The icons can be changed (or removed)

The 9-box matrix grid report functionality can also be used with other components. In Figure 9.23 we see another report that I am calling "How vs What Matrix".

186

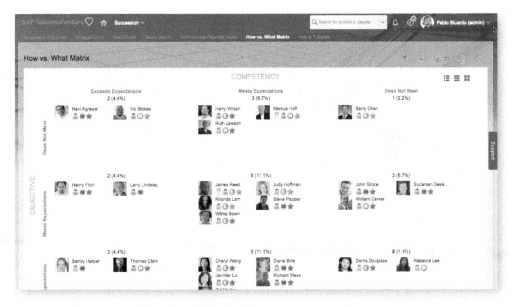

Figure 9.23: How vs What Matrix report

This report has a very similar format compared to our performance-potential matrix, but notice that I have removed the background colors of the boxes and of course this report is based on goals data (ratings) vs. competency data (ratings). It is up to each organization to define each axis of the report in a way that makes sense and adds value to the organization.

In summary this a very dynamic and interactive module that allows organization to track everything related to succession management. It offers very robust and user-friendly tools that can aid the succession planning process. Needless to say, pretty much all information seen up to this point can be reported.

Before we move into the next chapter, I would like to highlight again the deep integration between modules in SuccessFactors. In my opinion, that is one of the main reasons SuccessFactors can add so much value to an organization. When the system starts to gather, understand and display all talent data from all modules we have talked about, it can be extremely powerful at managing talent and making overall decisions.

I will leave you with a quick example that I personally had with one of my clients.

This was a Fortune 50 company. HR leaders started to utilize all the tools the succession management module offered to them, especially talent search and 9-box matrix grid reports.

They realized that minorities, in a particular location of the US, had very high overall performance and potential averages, and also were marked as high risk of loss for many of them. Of course these individuals were leaving the company rather quickly.

By leveraging SuccessFactors and data the system offered, they were able to establish a company-wide program to go above and beyond retaining individuals with high performance that could be a risk of leaving; including extra training (tracked in learning), development opportunities (development module), and of course additional compensation (compensation module).

I live and breathe examples like this, almost on a daily basis, with companies benefiting from all the data available in the system. It would take me several books to write about the empirical value, ROI and different metrics SuccessFactors can offer to any organization, but the key takeaway here is that information is a very powerful asset, and the fact that SuccessFactors slices and dices all talent data and makes it available to employees in the organization to help them make better decisions can be potentially huge at delivering value and running an organization better. At the end of the day, talent (people) is probably the most expensive asset in any organization.

Let's continue learning about one of the most important pieces in SuccessFactors, which is the security structure and role-based permissions.

10 Security structure

We are coming to the end of this overview of the talent management modules for part 1. You should now have a solid understanding of many of the talent management modules in SuccessFactors.

One very important item we have not covered yet is the security structure of the system. By security we mean what users can:

- ▶ Have access to (module and features)
- ▶ What they can read/view
- ▶ What they can write/edit
- ▶ What actions they can perform

I have not written much about security in each chapter because I wanted to dedicate a whole chapter to it before wrapping some things up.

In SuccessFactors there are two types of security structure:

1. Legacy security structure
2. Role-based permission (RBP)

In this book we will only focus on Role-based permission (RBP) because it is the recommended security structure, what 99% of customers have, and the only permission model that is actively supported by SuccessFactors and available to new customers.

10.1 Role-based permissions

Role-based permissions, known as RBP, manage permissions in SuccessFactors.

This suite-wide permission framework applies to all of the modules, with onboarding, learning and recruiting marketing having additional permission structures.

RBP can be found in Admin Center under Manage Employees as shown in Figure 10.1.

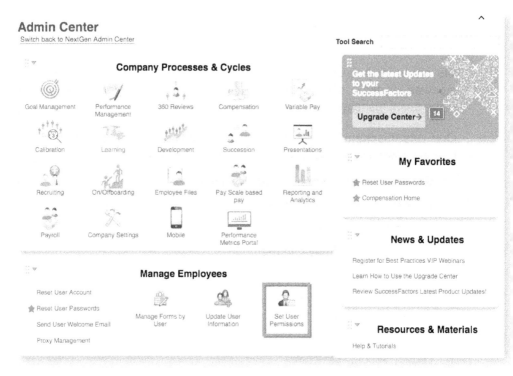

Figure 10.1: Access RBP in Admin Center

RBP is composed of permission groups and roles; let's learn more about these.

10.1.1 RBP groups

RBP groups are groups of people who share a common criteria. That's it, just a group of people.

Let's look at some examples. Let's begin by looking at Figure 10.2, which shows some of my permission groups in this system.

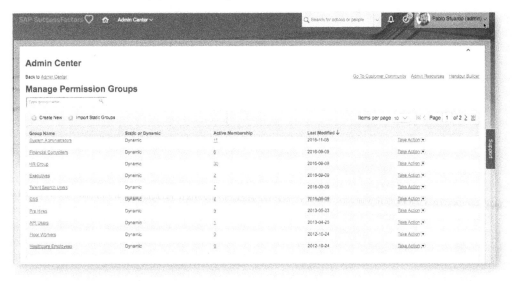

Figure 10.2: RBP permission group examples

If we look closely at Figure 10.2, we see there are different elements within these groups. Let's review some of them.

Group name

You probably guessed. Group names refer to the name of the group for your own reference. It is important to understand that RBP is a suite-wide framework, which among many things, means that all groups seen here will be visible and shared by all administrators with access to RBP.

In Figure 10.3 we see a closer look at the different groups I have in the system.

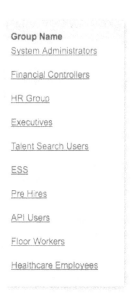

Figure 10.3: RBP group examples

We will explore some of these groups in more detail later in the chapter, but the key takeaway is that permission groups of people are based on different criteria and that should be reflected in the name. System Administrators clearly identifies the group of all system administrators in the system.

Static or dynamic

RBP groups can be static or dynamic. This is a simple, but powerful concept. Static groups mean that these cannot be modified (add or remove employees from the group), after the groups have initially been created.

Why would we want this? An example can be our integration owners. As an organization we might want to have a generic "admin" user (not a real user) who we know would never leave the organization, or get fired, nor be on leave, etc. This admin user will be the owner of all or integration jobs and APIs in the system and we don't want anyone to change this as it might have a very negative impact on integrations.

A dynamic group would be a group that can modified by adding or removing employees.

This is a very important concept. We might create a dynamic group to include all managers, or anyone who has direct reports. When someone gets promoted to a manager position, that person would automatically be added to the all managers group. Administrators would not have to go into RBP and add the person to the group every time.

Another example could be a recruiter. Let's say we have created a group to include anyone with the title Recruiter. Then if we just hired a person with a title of recruiter, the person would automatically be added to the group without needing an admin to add them to the group.

In Figure 10.4 we see how the system indicates whether a group is static or dynamic, as displayed right next to the group name.

Group Name	Static or Dynamic
System Administrators	Dynamic
Financial Controllers	Dynamic
HR Group	Dynamic
Executives	Dynamic
Talent Search Users	Dynamic
ESS	Dynamic
Pre Hires	Dynamic
API Users	Dynamic
Floor Workers	Dynamic
Healthcare Employees	Dynamic

Figure 10.4: Group name and dynamic or static

Active membership & last modified

Active membership just tells you the number of active users currently in the system (for that particular group). This is dynamic and if someone clicks on it, a new window will pop up with details about who is in the group as shown in Figure 10.5.

193

Figure 10.5: RBP group membership

Last modified let users know the last time the group (criteria) was modified. This can become quite handy to audit certain groups.

This information will be displayed next to static or dynamic as shown in Figure 10.6.

Static or Dynamic	Active Membership	Last Modified ↓
Dynamic	11	2016-11-08
Dynamic	6	2016-09-09
Dynamic	30	2016-09-09
Dynamic	2	2016-09-09
Dynamic	7	2016-09-09
Dynamic	2	2016-09-09
Dynamic	9	2013-05-23
Dynamic	1	2013-04-25
Dynamic	0	2012-10-24
Dynamic	0	2012-10-24

Figure 10.6: RBP groups, active membership and last modified

Take action

The last item of group basics is the menu for "Take Action" which can be found near the right of the screen as shown in Figure 10.7.

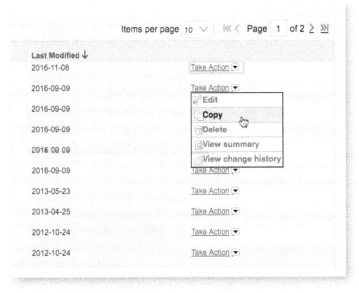

Figure 10.7: Take action within RBP groups

Within Take Action, there are several options for the admin user:

- ▶ **Edit group**: edit the group criteria.

- ▶ **Copy group**: copy the group and then modify it.

- ▶ **Delete group**: permanently delete groups.

- ▶ **View summary**: understand which RBP roles are associated with the group as shown in Figure 10.8.

- ▶ **View change history**: see the audit trail of the group. In other words see who has changed what historically with the group as shown in Figure 10.9.

Figure 10.8: View summary within take action in permission groups

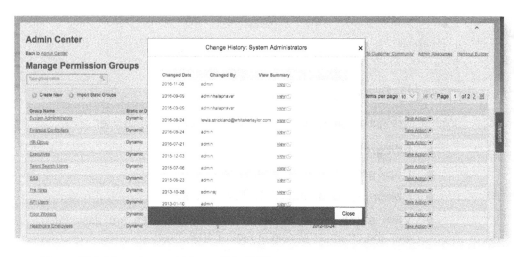

Figure 10.9: View change history within RBP groups

Let's look in detail at RBP groups next. Now that we have a better understanding of the basics of RBP groups, now we'll see how these are created.

Earlier we mentioned that RBP groups are based on different criteria. In Figure 10.10 we see how to select different people pools to define RBP groups.

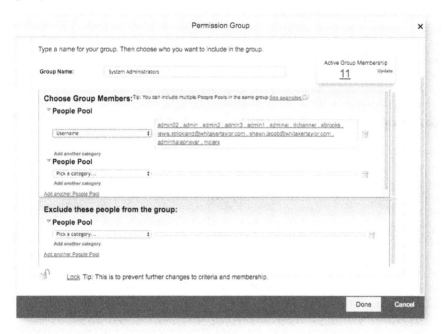

Figure 10.10: RBP group people pools

People pools define the criteria to be used to create the group. When we talk about criteria, we are referring to data fields that users are associated with. For example, if we would like to create a group with all females in the organization (because we would like to have only them see a field called "Maternity Leave"), we would select the field Gender to create the people pool like shown in Figure 10.11.

197

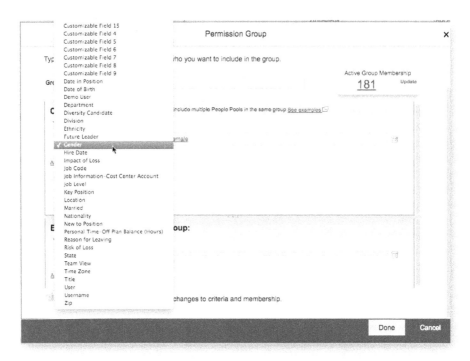

Figure 10.11: Data field selection for people pool in RBP group

At this point you should be asking yourself, where are these data fields coming from, and where is the information associated with this coming from?

The answer to is employee profile. All the data fields available to create groups are the exact same ones defined under the personal information sections in employee profile; and of course, whatever data each user has, is what groups will read from.

Let's review another example. Let's say we are putting together a group for all people identified as high risk of loss because we would like to show them extra learning opportunities and invite them to a special development program; but these should also have a value for high impact of loss, and we are only going to do it as a pilot for the marketing department.

If we take a look at Figure 10.12 we can see how this would be defined.

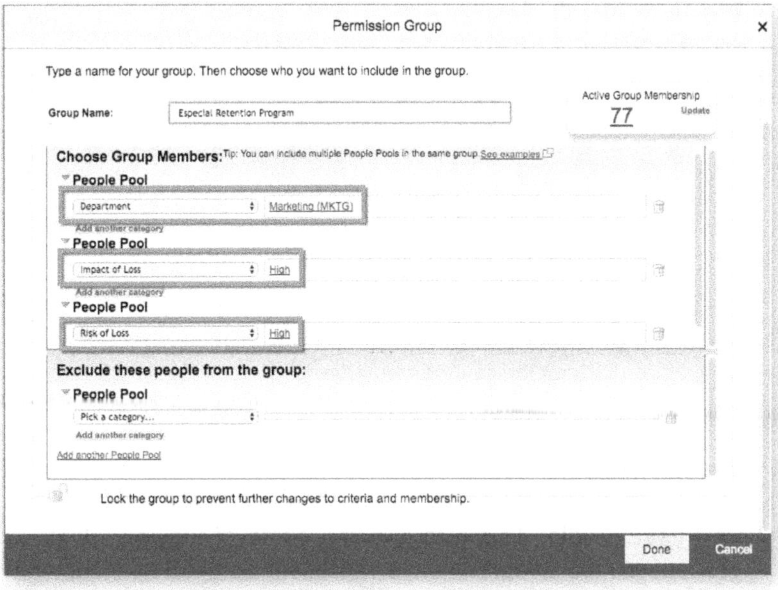

Figure 10.12: Define different people pools in RBP groups

Now that we have a clear understanding of RBP groups and how these are built, let's review how an admin grants authorization to these different groups by learning about RBP roles.

10.1.2 RBP roles

Earlier in the chapter we learned how to create RBP groups, which is essentially grouping users together based on different criteria. However, these groups are meaningless unless someone grants some type of authorization to them by associating them with RBP roles.

If we take a look at Figure 10.13 we can see that the summary screen looks very similar to RBP groups. Let's quickly review what each column means:

199

Figure 10.13: RBP roles

▶ **Permission role**: This refers to the name of the role. Just like groups, names should always represent something meaningful about the role.

▶ **Description**: This displays a description of each role. Roles can grant different types of access, so it is always important to offer extra information in the way of a description for an admin to have a complete understanding of the governance of the role.

▶ **Status**: Active or inactive. An active role is a role that has been associated with an RBP group. An inactive role is a role that has been created, but not been associated with an RBP group yet.

▶ **Last modified**: This displays the date of the last time the role was modified. This can become quite handy to audit certain roles.

▶ **Take action**: These are the exact same actions that can be done with RBP groups.

Permissions

Permission roles are composed of two sets of available permissions:

1. User permissions

2. Administrator permissions

User permissions include those that are potentially relevant to the entire user population, whereas administrator permissions only include authorizations that are relevant to administrators such as configuring a performance template.

If we look at Figure 10.14 we can see how we would grant permissions.

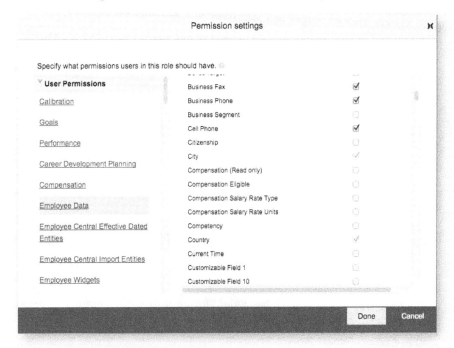

Figure 10.14: Grant RBP role authorizations

On the left side we can see different sets of authorizations that are self-explanatory. For example, I have selected "Employee Data"; therefore, on the right side of the screen different data fields belonging to the employee profile would display. I have selected the ones that I would like people to see.

Let's look at another example of user permissions. In Figure 10.15, I am granting access to features under the succession module.

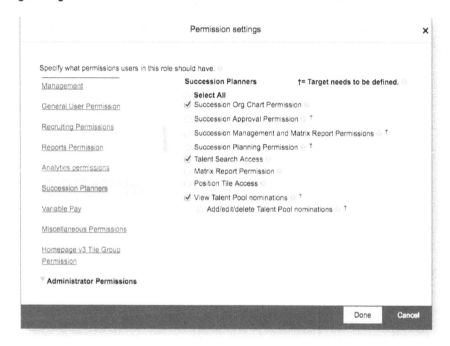

Figure 10.15: Authorization to access succession module

Under user permissions, I have selected the succession planners group and checked permissions for people to see the succession org chart, talent search, etc.

Looking closely at Figure 10.15, we can see that next to some authorization there is a little cross symbol. This symbol represents that particular authorization requires a target population to be defined.

As defined by SuccessFactors, a target population is a group of users whom this permission applies to. For example, if your organization has a number of departments, but you want administrator Ian to change user information only for department A, you would only grant authorization to Ian for a target population of department A.

Let's review an example of an administrator permission by looking at Figure 10.16.

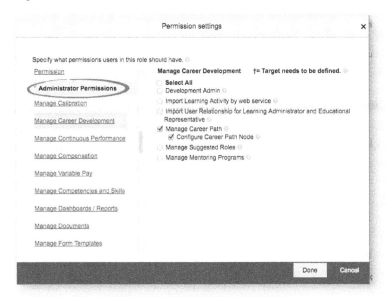

Figure 10.16: Administrator permission definition example

In this case, I have scrolled down, and under Administrator Permission, I can see all sets of authorizations for administrators.

In Figure 10.16 I have selected admin permissions for career development, and I am trying to grant access to someone to "Manage Career Path". Of course we do not want everyone in the organization, or a large number of individuals managing or changing the career paths.

Notice the different word "manage", which normally refers in Success-Factors to control and configure something, rather than just simply accessing. For access to career path, the authorization would be found under user permissions, since we probably would want a large number of users to take advantage of it.

10.1.3 Role and group relationship

The last concept to understand in this Role-based permission model is the relationship between groups and roles.

We already understand how groups are composed by people based on different criteria, and that in roles, admins define the actual permissions. These permissions are meaningless if we don't assign them, or grant them to someone (group of people).

With RBP after we have defined our set of permissions, we would grant those authorization to a permission group. For example, if we would like all users to have access to the goals management we would have to:

▶ Create a permission group that includes all users

▶ Create a permission role that includes the authorization to access goals management

▶ Grant this permission role to the appropriate permission group

In Figure 10.17 we see how this would look.

Figure 10.17: Grant roles to permission groups

We see that in this case I have granted this role (or all authorizations previously defined), to be permission groups "Everyone (All Employees)" and "ESS".

Notice that there is a column for target population. As discussed earlier, there are some authorizations that require a target population. In the case of Figure 10.17 we are granting all permissions (defined earlier) to the group ESS, and they have those permissions (that require target population) over a permission group for All (Employees).

Another use case could be when we would only want managers to see performance reviews of their direct reports and no one else. In this case we would grant the authorization to see performance reviews for permission group "All Managers" and target population "Only Direct Reports".

In summary, Role-based permission is critical in SuccessFactors. It is how the entire security structure is handled

Like many other items within SuccessFactors, it would take an entire book to go over all the hundreds of potential permissions that can be given, and what they mean, but this introduction and overview, is a huge stepping stone to learning RBP and will help you tremendously if and when you decide to embrace SuccessFactors.

As always, a note regarding security. RBP is probably the most powerful tool administrators have over the system, so security governance should be treated with lots of care.

I have seen cases where RBP has been handled lightly and it has turned into complete disasters—everyone running reports on compensation data and performance data for the entire organization—just one example of many I have seen in my years of experience.

We are almost coming to the end of this introduction to SuccessFactors part one, but next we will learn about one of the most important modules in the platform, which is general reporting.

11 Reporting

We are approaching the end of this book (Part 1). By this time you should have a very clear idea of what SuccessFactors is, and what is does through its different modules.

We already understand that the talent suite for SuccessFactors can pretty much support all processes related to this important business function through its very interactive and dynamic approach; however, in my opinion, for talent management practices, almost everything is pretty much useless unless we can report on all that data that we have been collecting in each module.

Now I will introduce you to the basic reporting capabilities of the platform, which includes ad-hoc reporting and dashboards. As mentioned earlier, basic reporting belongs to the system platform, so any client who purchases a license for at least one module would have access to these capabilities.

SuccessFactors has a whole suite of reporting capabilities, which includes online report designer, workforce analytics and workforce planning. These are way out of the scope of this book, but I invite you to learn more about what these reporting modules can offer.

Let's begin understanding these basic reporting capabilities with ad-hoc reports.

11.1 Ad-hoc reports

Ad-hoc reports in its most basic form allows users to report essentially all data captured in the system in a columns and rows type of format (very similar to Excel).

Users would access the reporting module from the home menu as always, and then clicking Reports as shown in Figure 11.1.

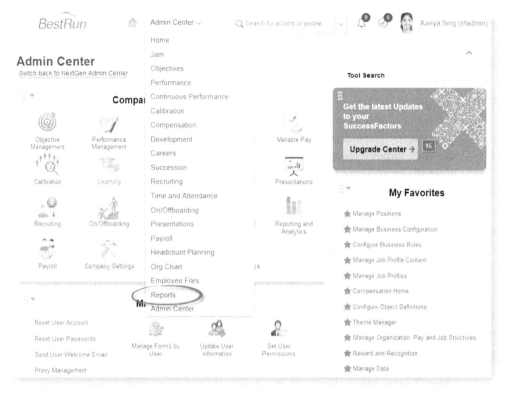

Figure 11.1: Accessing reporting

Once accessed, the user will be taken to the reports home page. On the left side of the screen, users can see (Figure 11.2):

▶ Pre-packaged reports under reports center

▶ Any saved ad-hoc reports

▶ Any reports that have been scheduled

▶ The ad-hoc report builder

▶ Standard reports

Figure 11.2: Reporting home page

Let's learn more about these.

11.1.1 Report center reports

Every platform comes with pre-packaged reports. These reports cannot be modified and only work if standard fields have been used in different modules (there are almost no reason not to use standard fields).

Let's review some of these delivered reports starting with some of the list view reports.

List view reports

If we look at Figure 11.3, we see how a list report looks.

209

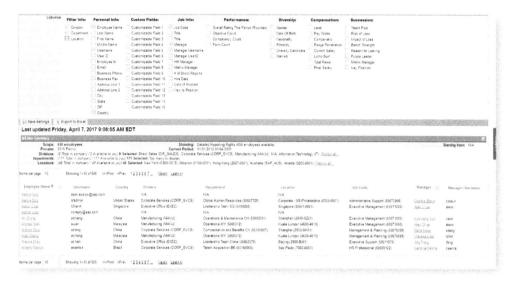

Figure 11.3: List view example

As you can see, list view reports lists of data. In this case, I ran a report about general employee information.

On top we can see how the user can select which columns to display. Needless to say, all information seen here comes from other modules. Here we have information from employee profile (personal information), performance, compensation and succession.

If we look toward the middle of Figure 11.3 we can see that the reports gives a summary of the data.

At the bottom the user gets to see the actual results of the report. These reports can be:

▶ Sorted

▶ Filtered

▶ Exported to Excel

I will mention again that unfortunately you cannot modify these reports. You can filter and choose which data to display, but that's about the flexibility available.

Let's look at another example of a list view report. If we look at Figure 11.4, we see a list view report related to competencies.

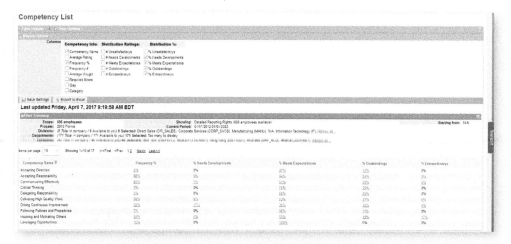

Figure 11.4: Competencies list view report

In the very same fashion at the last report we looked at, here we can select which columns to display (related to competencies), and we see a summary of the report with the actual results.

Now that we understand more about list view reports, let's learn about spotlight views.

Spotlight view Reports

Spotlight reports are a bit more dynamic. These reports focus on showing users more targeted and overall information, rather than a whole list of data.

Figure 11.5: Spotlight view report example

If we look at Figure 11.5, we can see how the report is a graph rather than a full list of data. In this case, I ran the competency breakdown spotlight report to understand where the organization stands for different competencies.

These can be very interesting. Let's say an HR leader who sees that the competency with the lower ratings in Leveraging Opportunities. Based on this information, she should start painting the picture that perhaps the culture of the organization doesn't encourage taking opportunities and risk.

The last report types under report center is classic reports.

Classic reports

Classic reports are very similar to list view reports. It displays a list of data that can be filtered and exported.

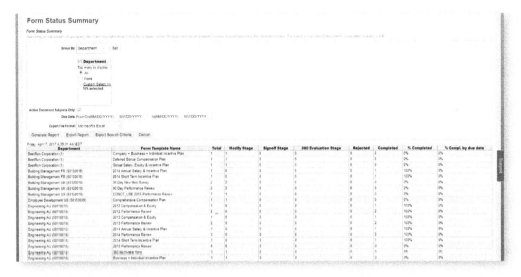

Figure 11.6: Form status summary classic report

If we look at Figure 11.6 we can see that this particular report tells the user in which step of the process performance forms are. If you look at each column, that represents a step in the route map of performance forms. These reports can be exported too.

As you can see under the report center, there are about a dozen pre-delivered reports. To tell you the truth, these reports are not very commonly used because with the capabilities that we are about to see next, the same data can be reported in a much more flexible format.

Let's review ad-hoc reports next.

11.1.2 Ad-hoc reports

Ad-hoc reports allow users to report on data from all different data sets (modules).

213

Figure 11.7: Ad-hoc report home page

If we look at Figure 11.7 we can see a list of reports. All these reports were created by this particular user.

Before we see how the actual report looks, I would like to mention that ad-hoc reports can be:

► Run online (to view the data in the application itself without the need to download a file)

► Exported to Excel

► Exported as PDF document or PPT presentation

► Shared with other users

If we look at Figure 11.8 we can see how an ad-hoc report looks. In this case I built a report to look at users, department and cost centers. All the columns you see in this report were selected by me once I created the report.

An important point to keep in mind is that these columns can be obtained from all different modules. Each column represents a field in a module. I would say about 99% of information in SuccessFactors can be reported.

All this information can be filtered and sorted before being processed, such that when you run a report, it comes ready as the data you are interested on.

214

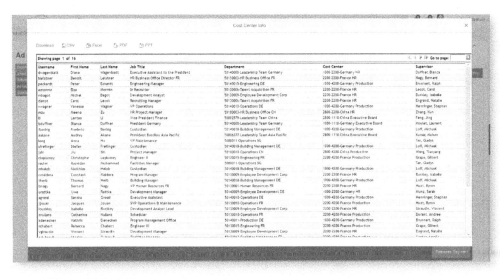

Figure 11.8: Ad-hoc report example

Let's take a look at another example.

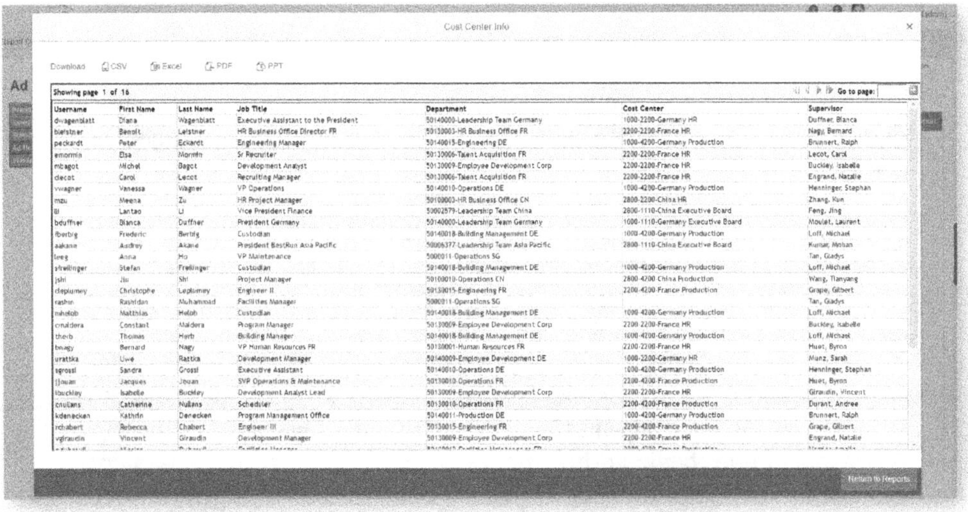

Figure 11.9: Employee demographics ad-hoc report

In Figure 11.9 I created a report about employee demographics. Again, I selected the columns, their order, and filters.

If I decided to export this report to Excel, I would simply click on the Excel button at the top and export it (Figure 11.10).

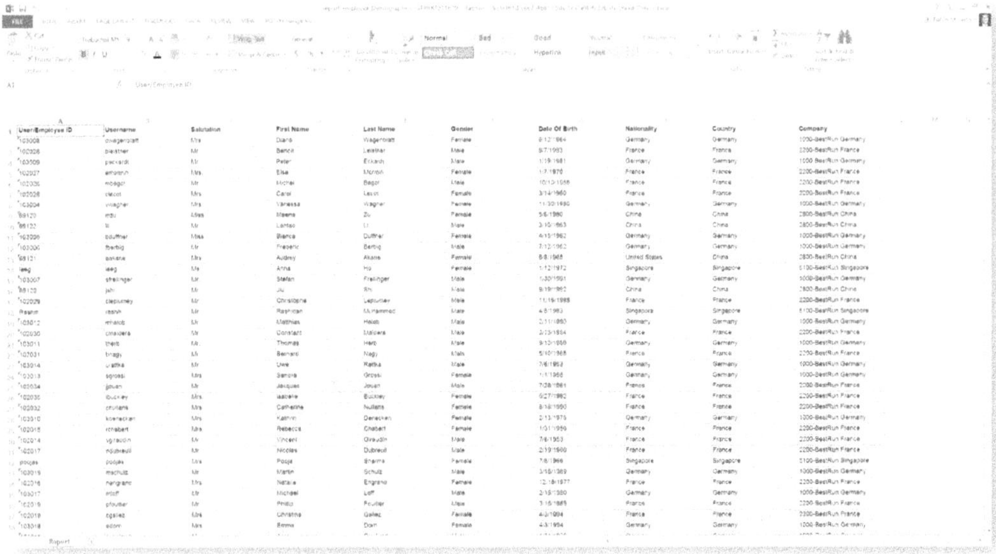

Figure 11.10: Export ad-hoc reports to MS Excel

There is no limit to the number of columns a report can have, the number of modules involved in the report nor the number of reports a single user can have.

Like mentioned earlier, reports can be shared with other users or groups in addition to being able to schedule reports. This can come in very handy for those HR business partners that are tasked to send reports to leadership on a pre-determined time frequency (daily, weekly, etc.).

Ad-hoc reports are extremely flexible to accommodate basically any reporting needs your organization might have, but I will say that no logic is available under basic ad-hoc reporting. When I say logic, I mean concatenating field data, creating "If" statements, and other logic; however, this is supported by online report designer, which is a separate module out of the scope of this book.

Now that we have an understanding of ad-hoc reports and its ability to report on basically any data available in the system from any module, let's learn more about dashboards.

216

11.1.3 Dashboards

Dashboards are a functionality that belongs to the basic reporting eco-system in the SuccessFactors platform, and basically reports data in graphs instead of lists (columns).

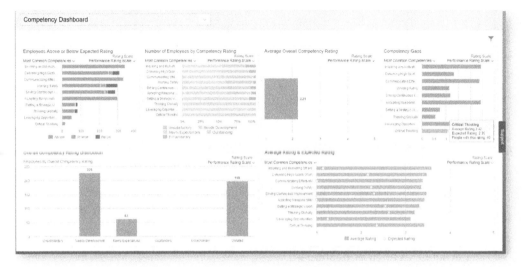

Figure 11.11: Competency dashboard

If we look at Figure 11.11, we can see how user-friendly and engaging these graphs are.

In this case I ran my competency dashboard, which of course has information all about competencies. Each tile (or graph) you see in the screen is configurable, which means you can change the data that is being reported (X or Y axis), colors, position, etc.

Not only that, but these dashboards can also be filtered, for example. If we have a President of one division that only cares about his division, when we build the graphs, we can define this in such a way that users only see data related to them.

In addition, if we would like to understand at an even deeper level, we can click on a bar itself, and the values that make up the bar on each graph display as shown in Figure 11.12.

Figure 11.12: Detail data in dashboards

Notice that I clicked on the critical thinking competency at the very bottom of the graph, and the values that make up that bar display at the bottom.

Let's look at another dashboard.

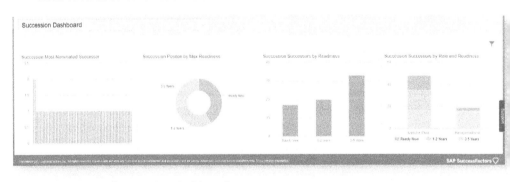

Figure 11.13: Succession dashboard

If we look at Figure 11.13, I ran my succession dashboard that reports succession data.

Notice that the second graph is a pie chart rather than bars. Success-Factors dashboards support:

▶ Bar charts

▶ Pie charts

▶ Line chart

If we stay with that chart (succession position by max readiness), and I click on 1-2 Years (green data), the information about what composes that data displays at the bottom of the screen (Figure 11.14).

Figure 11.14: Details information in dashboards

Figure 11.15: Performance and competencies dashboard

If we look at Figure 11.15, which is another dashboard example, I would like to point out a few other things:

▶ The name of the dashboards and graphs (tiles) can be changed and customized

▶ The colors can be customized to match your company culture

▶ There is no limit to the number of graphs (tiles) that you can have for each particular dashboard

▶ You can include graphs with data from different modules in a single dashboard

▶ There is no limit to the number of dashboards each user might have

▶ Dashboards can be share among users and groups

▶ Anybody (with the right authorizations) can create their own dashboards

▶ Dashboards are mobile-enabled

▶ Dashboards can be shared in a SuccessFactors home page as a tile.

With those key points I'd like to finish by saying that dashboards are an incredible tool and very popular with executives. Users can report data form all modules and truthfully creativity is the limit. These dashboards can be created literally in minutes, and do not require any additional technical skill.

11.2 Final remarks

Writing this book has been an extremely rewarding experience. I will intimately admit that it leaves an empty feeling not being able to showcase and explain every single capability, feature and functionality of each module reviewed. This would take at a minimum a single book per module.

Having said that, on the positive note, I truthfully believe that the concepts and information presented in this book is enough for anyone to learn the basics and be educated at least on what SuccessFactors is, what it does, and how it can benefit your organization.

As mentioned in the introduction, this book is part one of a series of two books. In this first part, we covered all modules related to performance & alignment, and total reward.

In book two of this series, we will focus on recruiting execution, which includes the modules of recruiting management, recruiting marketing and onboarding, in addition to going over the learning module.

I want to repeat something I mentioned in the succession chapter. It would take me several books to write about the empirical value, ROI and different metrics SuccessFactors can offer to organization, but the key takeaway here is that information is a very powerful asset. The fact that SuccessFactors slices and dices all talent data and makes it available to leaders and HR customers in the organization to help them make better decisions, can be potentially huge at delivering value. This being a critical component at navigating the transformative age we live in.

At the end of the day, talent (people) is probably the most expensive asset in any organization.

I sincerely hope you enjoyed reading this book and learned about the exciting ecosystem of SuccessFactors. I hope you have a full understanding of what SuccessFactors is and which solutions it can offer to common HR business problems in the talent management framework.

ESPRESSO TUTORIALS

You have finished the book.

A The Author

Pablo Stuardo belongs to the Advisory Services : practice of Ernst & Young LLP. Pablo specializes on HR Cloud Technologies, in particular SAP SuccessFactors. He has participated successfully in numerous SuccessFactors end-to-end implementations and has successfully delivered North American implementations as well global roll outs. Within these projects, he has played many roles, from leading the full implementation, to project management, to functional and technical lead resources, leveraging his deep technical skills, in addition to his broad experience with SuccessFactors.

Originally from Chile, Pablo is fluent in English and Spanish.

B Index

C   Disclaimer

This publication contains references to the products of SAP SE.

SAP, R/3, SAP NetWeaver, Duet, PartnerEdge, ByDesign, SAP BusinessObjects Explorer, StreamWork, and other SAP products and services mentioned herein as well as their respective logos are trademarks or registered trademarks of SAP SE in Germany and other countries.

Business Objects and the Business Objects logo, BusinessObjects, Crystal Reports, Crystal Decisions, Web Intelligence, Xcelsius, and other Business Objects products and services mentioned herein as well as their respective logos are trademarks or registered trademarks of Business Objects Software Ltd. Business Objects is an SAP company.

Sybase and Adaptive Server, iAnywhere, Sybase 365, SQL Anywhere, and other Sybase products and services mentioned herein as well as their respective logos are trademarks or registered trademarks of Sybase, Inc. Sybase is an SAP company.

SAP SE is neither the author nor the publisher of this publication and is not responsible for its content. SAP Group shall not be liable for errors or omissions with respect to the materials. The only warranties for SAP Group products and services are those that are set forth in the express warranty statements accompanying such products and services, if any. Nothing herein should be construed as constituting an additional warranty.

More Espresso Tutorials Books

Björn Weber:

First Steps in the SAP® Production Processes (PP)

▶ Compact manual for discrete production in SAP

▶ Comprehensive example with numerous illustrations

▶ Master data, resource planning and production orders in context

http://5027.espresso-tutorials.com

Sydnie McConnell & Martin Munzel:

First Steps in SAP® (2nd, extended edition)

▶ Learn how to navigate in SAP ERP

▶ Learn about transactions, organizational units, master data

▶ Watch instructional videos with simple, step-by-step examples

▶ Get an overview of SAP products and new development trends

http://5045.espresso-tutorials.com

Ashish Sampat:

First Steps in SAP® Controlling (CO)

▶ Cost center and product cost planning and actual cost flow

▶ Best practices for cost absorption using Product Cost Controlling

▶ Month-end closing activities in SAP Controlling

▶ Examples and screenshots based on a case study approach

http://5069.espresso-tutorials.com

Ann Cacciottolli:

First Steps in SAP® Financial Accounting (FI)

▶ Overview of key SAP Financials functionality and SAP ERP integration

▶ Step-by-step guide to entering transactions

▶ SAP Financials reporting capabilities

▶ Hands-on instruction based on examples and screenshots

http://5095.espresso-tutorials.com

Janet Salmon & Claus Wild:

First Steps in SAP® S/4HANA Finance

▶ Understand the basics of SAP S/4HANA Finance

▶ Explore the new architecture, configuration options, and SAP Fiori

▶ Examine SAP S/4HANA Finance migration steps

▶ Assess the impact on business processes

http://5149.espresso-tutorials.com

Claudia Jost:

First Steps in the SAP® Purchasing Processes (MM), Second Edition

► Step-by-step instructions for creating a vendor master record and a purchase requisition

► How to convert a purchase requisition to a purchase order

► Approval process and credit approval procedure fundamentals

► Tips on how to create favorites

http://5166.espresso-tutorials.com/

Bert Vanstechelman:

The SAP® HANA Deployment Guide

► SAP HANA sizing, capacity planning guidelines, and data tiering

► Deployment options and data provisioning scenarios

► Backup and recovery options and procedures

► Software and hardware virtualization in SAP HANA

http://5289.espresso-tutorials.com